MW00587197

FRAMING FLYNN

FRAMING FLYNN

THE SCANDALOUS TAKEDOWN OF AN AMERICAN GENERAL

DAVE ERICKSON

A POST HILL PRESS BOOK
ISBN: 978-1-64293-729-9
ISBN (eBook): 978-1-64293-730-5

Framing Flynn:
The Scandalous Takedown of an American General

Cover art by Cody Corcoran

Photo of Michael Flynn by Saul Loeb/AFP via Getty Images

Post Hill Press
New York • Nashville
posthillpress.com

Published in the United States of America
1 2 3 4 5 6 7 8 9 10

CONTENTS

"Though they plot evil against you, and devise wicked schemes, they cannot succeed."

—Psalms 21:11

FOREWORD

THE LEGAL PERSECUTION OF GENERAL MICHAEL FLYNN IS the Rosetta Stone that permits us to understand the coup d'état treason planned in January 2017 at the highest levels of the Obama regime to remove President Donald Trump, a duly elected president, from office.

Appointed by President Trump to be the twenty-fourth national security advisor in the White House, Flynn had to be removed by the coup d'état traitors in the CIA, the DOJ, and the FBI, before he had a chance to use his extensive intelligence capabilities to expose Hillary Clinton and Barack Obama as Number 1 and Number 2 leading the regime-change cabal. Now declassified documents, including a handwritten note by former FBI official Peter Strzok, made clear that on January 5, 2017—fifteen days before President Trump's inauguration—President Obama presided over an Oval Office meeting attended by Vice President Joe Biden, then-FBI Director James Comey, National Security Advisor Susan Rice, and

Deputy Attorney General Sally Yates. At that meeting, the scheme was concocted for the FBI to entrap General Flynn so he could be indicted for "lying to the FBI" over a conversation Flynn had conducted with Russian Ambassador Sergey Kislyak in December 2016. That conversation was a perfectly acceptable responsibility of General Flynn in the transition to the incoming Trump administration. We now know the major subject was an anti-Israel United Nations resolution on Israel being promoted by President Obama as his final assault against Prime Minister Netanyahu in Obama's final weeks in office. Despite abundant evidence that the FBI did not believe Flynn lied, Strzok allowed his political animus against Trump to overrule his professional judgment as he supervised the counter-intelligence investigation that forced General Flynn to plead guilty to an offense Flynn never committed.

Attorney Sidney Powell waged an epic battle to contest General Flynn's guilty plea. Through a series of courageous briefs filed in Flynn's federal district court criminal case, Powell established that Washington-based law firm Covington & Burling gave Powell incompetent advice on registering under the Foreign Agent Registration Act (FARA) for which Covington (the law firm of former Attorney General Eric Holder) billed Flynn millions of dollars in legal fees. She revealed emails that documented that Covington made errors advising Flynn in his FARA filing, hid exculpatory evidence from Flynn, and urged

Flynn to accept the guilty plea to block Mueller's attack dogs from prosecuting his son.

Among the shocking revelations in the Flynn case are the cozy revolving-door relationships that exist between the federal bureaucracy and the establishment Washington law firms that are a lucrative retirement parking place for Department of Justice prosecutors. "I have devoted my life to my country, only to be accused of crimes, slandered in the media with false and misleading claims, and have my family threatened—all an unimaginable nightmare—one only those who have not walked in my shoes will find difficult to comprehend," Flynn argued, asserting the truth that his prosecution was yet another outrage committed by Obama officials in the DOJ and FBI whose goal was to weaponize our justice system against political enemies. Truly, the criminals in the Flynn case are the Mueller prosecutors who put a gun to the head of Flynn's son and threatened to pull the trigger unless Flynn signed their guilty plea.

These Mueller prosecutors also attempted to suborn perjury in my case, threatening me that I would spend the rest of my life in a federal prison unless I agreed to say I had a contact with Julian Assange and Wikileaks that I shared with the Trump campaign. As I detailed in my book, *Silent No More: How I Became a Political Prisoner of Mueller's "Witch Hunt,"* I refused to take the corrupt Mueller deal, unable to stand before a federal judge and before God to swear to a crime I did not commit. I was never prosecuted, a fact that shows the corruption of the pressure Mueller's

Office of Special Counsel was willing to exert simply to prove their "Russian Collusion" conspiracy theory—a lie the DOJ and FBI knew was little more than Russian disinformation from the start.

Powell's determined requests that the DOJ and FBI turn over exculpatory evidence finally resulted in Attorney General Barr withdrawing all criminal charges in Flynn's case, effectively throwing out the two guilty pleas Flynn had given in federal criminal case. But instead of ending the case right there, Federal District Judge Emmett Sullivan refused to dismiss Flynn's case, insisting he as judge and jury still had the right to continue judicial hearings on sentencing Flynn to a crime for which the Department of Justice was no longer charging him. Judge Sullivan's behavior in the Flynn case reveals clearly that politically motivated judges have thrown away our Constitutional rights to "equal justice under law," as they punish their political enemies with socialist "Lawfare" maneuvers unprecedented in the long history of United States jurisprudence. But Justice Sullivan's perfidy did not end there. Unwilling to accept a dismissal of Flynn's criminal case by a three-judge panel of the Federal Circuit Court of Appeals, Judge Sullivan demanded a full en banc hearing before the Circuit Court. With the Circuit Court referring the case back to Judge Sullivan, the case dragged on. By refusing to abide by established U.S. criminal procedure, Judge Sullivan, with the complicity of the U.S. Circuit Court of Appeals, managed to silence Flynn until after the presidential election on November 3, 2020.

By inventing law from the bench, Judge Sullivan revealed himself to be yet another cancer at the heart of U.S. justice under Hillary Clinton and Barack Obama's radicalized political left.

Sullivan showed he was a leftist judge that apparently did not see the need for a criminal indictment to render a criminal sentence on a legitimate American hero whose only crime was to support Donald Trump. But with the U.S. DOJ and FBI acting like Hitler's Gestapo or Stalin's KGB, why should we expect anything different than a Hitler/Stalin "show trial" from a "Trump Derangement Syndrome" federal judiciary?

Dave Erickson's important book details exactly how and why the Obama administration Deep State agents framed General Flynn. Put simply, the Obama White House, about to leave office in January 2017, was desperately afraid that Flynn as national security advisor to President Trump would reveal the many crimes committed by Barack Obama, Joe Biden, and Hillary Clinton in conducting U.S. foreign policy for their personal enrichment. Obama, Biden, and Clinton have never explained many unsolved foreign policy mysteries.

- Why was Ambassador Chris Stevens in Benghazi on September 11, 2012, without the protection he begged to be put into place?
- Why were pallets of cash flown to Iran in U.S. military cargo airplanes as part of a fraudulent Obama administration deal that allowed Iran to build nuclear weapons after a waiting period?
- Why did the Obama administration encourage, organize, and fund the uprisings under the Arab Spring that allowed the Muslim Brotherhood to take power in Egypt while Islamic radicals toppled the Qaddafi regime in Libya?
- Why was ISIS armed by Hillary Clinton illegally shipping weapons through Libya and Turkey to the so-called ISIS "rebels" in Syria?

Nor do we know why Barack Obama allowed Joe Biden through his son, Hunter, to be paid millions from a fraudulent energy firm in Ukraine?

Why did Hunter Biden fly with his father on Air Force 2 to China? How did Hunter Biden secure a billion-dollar investment deal from the Communist Party ruling China that benefitted Chinese companies anxious to expand their market presence in the United States? Or why was the Clinton Foundation allowed to receive millions of dollars of "donations" from Canadian investors who benefited while Hillary Clinton steered through regulatory hurdles the sale of 20 percent of U.S. uranium to Russia under the crooked Uranium One deal?

Given what Obama, Clinton, and Biden knew of the crimes they had committed conducting U.S. foreign policy for personal gain, the risk General Flynn would expose these crimes was too much for the Obama-Clinton-Biden cabal to bear. Thus, the destruction of General Flynn's career through framing him for the crime of lying to the FBI was a small price these coup d'état traitors were willing to commit to preserve their foreign policy cover-up. Hence, General Flynn became collateral damage as the DOJ/FBI "insurance policy" to impeach President Trump transitioned from Operation Crossfire Hurricane to the Mueller investigation. Now, the goal was to silence Flynn in order to cover up the coup d'état plan to use "Russian collusion"—a hoax we now know

Hillary Clinton concocted—to make sure Donald Trump would never serve out his term despite being the legitimately elected president of the United States. Suffering his ordeal at the hands of these criminals and traitors, General Flynn lost his home to pay his legal bills, suffered four years under threat of going to prison, and had his stellar military career tarnished all because he knew, or would most certainly have found out, where Obama, Hillary, and Biden had buried the corpses.

I applaud Dave Erickson for bringing this information forth, and I urge you to read this book not only with attention but also with alarm. Except for heroes like General Flynn and attorney Sidney Powell, we might yet lose this Republic and our Constitutional freedoms to a group of Democrat Marxists who are desperate for power at any cost—even the cost of committing treason. I believe this book beautifully chronicles the injustices perpetrated on an American patriot—a man who'd ultimately be pardoned by President Trump, and rightfully receive the vindication and the justice he so richly deserved.

—Jerome R. Corsi, PhD

PREFACE

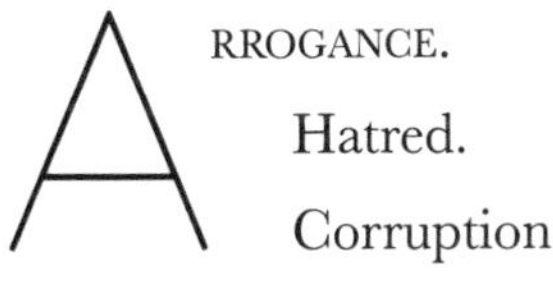

ARROGANCE.

Hatred.

Corruption.

Vindictiveness.

These are the cornerstones on which this story is built. A true tale of good versus evil.

I didn't know the extent of the evil when my publisher asked if I'd be interested in writing about the Flynn case. I knew Flynn had been railroaded but wasn't anywhere close to knowing the depths to which corrupt actors would sink to push a lie—and how they'd use that lie to destroy people's lives. Nor did I know just how high up in the government the evil went.

The takedown of Lieutenant General Michael Flynn, with the vile, reprobate, and often illegal behavior of agents from the Federal Bureau of Investigation, their bosses—heavy-hitters in the Obama administration—Joe Biden, and Barack

Obama himself, is the most heinous miscarriage of justice and biggest political scandal in the history of American politics.

Oh, one could cite the night of June 17, 1972, when GOP operatives broke into the headquarters of the Democratic National Committee at the Watergate complex in Washington, DC, as being worse. The break-in and ensuing investigation opened a Pandora's box of corruption and exposed a trail of bad acts leading straight to the Oval Office. "Watergate," which ultimately took down President Richard Nixon and sent other politicos to prison has, for the better part of nearly fifty years, been the benchmark by which all corruption and scandal is measured.

Not anymore.

Watergate is amateur-hour tomfoolery carried out by the Apple Dumpling Gang compared to the organized criminal enterprise orchestrated and executed at the highest levels of government to destroy Donald Trump, his staff, and ultimately, his presidency.

The effort to link them all to Russia—that they were conspiring with a foreign government—is so ridiculously absurd it would be laughable if it wasn't so spine-chillingly terrifying that it happened in the United States of America.

No one aligned with Trump was safe from crooked truth-assassins armed with a grudge and a badge.

Before I wade knee-deep into the swampy marsh detailing the actions of corrupt government officials, a few things must be made clear. Despite what Special Counsel Robert Mueller, former FBI Director James Comey, a few rogue agents, and a complicit biased media have tried to make you believe—

Michael Flynn committed no crime.

His phone call with a Russian ambassador named Sergey Kislyak was not a crime.

What was discussed during that call was not a crime.

What he told the FBI was not a crime.

How he described the call to Vice President Mike Pence was not a crime.

If my point hasn't been made, then I'll make it more succinct—Michael Flynn committed no crime.

It's just such a sad statement on where we are today as a country that Flynn is vilified as a criminal on one side and hailed, rightfully, as a falsely-accused patriot on the other. This is division fueled by a two-term president from Chicago with a Marxist agenda and a lack of American values. It's to embrace a value system that says, "Do what I say, not what I do." A system of the entitled that takes what it wants regardless of cost. It is envy. It is jealousy. It is separation by race and class. And it lusts for power at all costs without concern for who gets hurt along the way.

That's the system that took down Flynn and so many others before, and after, Trump became president. The Left and its propaganda arm—the mainstream national news media, composed of left-wing activists disguised as "journalists"—propagated the farcical notion Flynn had an alliance with Russians—that he's some sort of subversive operating at the whim of a duplicitous madman. And by madman, they don't mean Putin, they mean Trump.

When I decided to tackle this project, I knew the basic bullet points of the Flynn case:

- As incoming national security advisor, Flynn had a phone conversation with a Russian ambassador.
- Flynn was accused of asking Russia not to retaliate for the sanctions Obama levied against it.
- When questioned about the call, the FBI claimed Flynn lied both to investigators and to Pence about what he said.
- He pleaded guilty to lying to the FBI—even though he never lied about anything.
- After some legal wrangling, documents were released that proved there was a coordinated plot by corrupt FBI agents to destroy Trump, Flynn, advisors Carter Page and George Papadopoulos, and campaign manager Paul Manafort.
- According to released Oval Office meeting notes, Barack Obama and Joe Biden not only knew about the plan to destroy Flynn, they were there when it was birthed.

- Flynn dumped his ineffective counsel, hired Sidney Powell, and took back his "guilty" plea.
- The Department of Justice, given all the evidence it now had at its disposal, decided against moving forward with the case against Flynn.
- An activist judge named Emmet Sullivan, despite the DOJ's decision to drop the case, ignored them and a federal appeals court ordering it be dismissed, and instead decided to make himself a party to it, keeping Flynn twisting in the wind.

What I didn't know was what I didn't know. Wow, there was a lot I didn't know. There are many arms to this complicated web of deceit—an elaborate frame job is many-layered. I poured through a seemingly endless mountain of research, and the more I studied, the more I determined the conspirators who framed Flynn hated Trump more than they loved America—if they even love America at all. What they really love is power. But dollars to donuts, it's not so much about their hatred as it is about their fear. These people feared what Trump would do—enacting policies to restore American ideals and disrupting the burgeoning wave of progressivism.

That's why they tried so hard to undermine him, without ever once considering, or caring, what their insatiable thirst to annihilate Trump would do to the country.

The plot against Flynn was part of a bigger anti-Trump agenda. Flynn wasn't the sole focus at first, but outside of Trump, he was the most important "get." So, while I do go into the specifics of his takedown, I've also laid out the overall big picture and tried to explain where he fits in it. The Russian collusion investigation was a comprehensive, global mission with an extraordinary number of players and details—some so complicated and not all that important to the story, so in a few places, I've painted the narrative with a wide brush to keep it from being slogged under an overwhelming amount of minutia. Hopefully, it's as uncomplicated and as easily digestible as I've tried to make it.

INTRODUCTION

IMAGINE A SCRIPT FOR A NEW HOLLYWOOD SPY THRILLER. SET during the infancy of the Cold War, the plot involves framing a newcomer to the Kremlin by the highest-ranking members of the Soviet Union's People's Commissariat for Internal Affairs, also known as NKVD, the police agency that mostly operated in secret engaging in political repression of innocent people, that usually resulted in either execution or a one-way trip to the Gulag. The newcomer is a highly decorated general in the Red Army, who'd faithfully served under the General Secretary of the Communist Party, Joseph Stalin, until Stalin fired him. He's returning as an advisor to an incoming high-ranking official whom Stalin hates with a passion. So, the NKVD, loyal to Stalin, and at Stalin's behest, launches a subversive plan to frame the general, faithfully mirroring the mantra of its leader, Lavrentiy Beria, "Show me the man and I'll show you the crime." Now, like hunters catching brown bear in the Kamchatka Peninsula, they set a trap and waited for the general to take the bait.

Ooh, sounds juicy! Tom Clancy on Line 1!

ACT ONE

FADE IN:

EXT: LUBYANKA SQUARE – DAY

DISSOLVE TO:

INT: MEETING ROOM – NKVD HEADQUARTERS. Inside the meeting room, the three most powerful men in the NKVD—the director, also known as the PEOPLE'S COMMISSAR OF THE INTERIOR, his deputy, formally called the DIRECTOR OF STATE SECURITY, and the HEAD OF COUNTERINTELLIGENCE.

HEAD OF COUNTERINTELLIGENCE
What's our goal? Truth/Admission or to get him to lie, so we can prosecute him or get him fired?

PEOPLE'S COMMISSAR OF THE INTERIOR

If we're seen as playing games, the Kremlin will be furious.

DIRECTOR OF STATE SECURITY

OK, so here's what we do. There's a law from 1799. It's so old, it was signed by Paul the First. I mean, it's never used, but it says if you're a Russian citizen, you can't correspond with an agent of a foreign government. Now, we know this law is vague, it's ancient, it should have been repealed ages ago, and that this guy, well, he didn't actually do anything wrong, but if we get him to admit to breaking that law, seriously, get *him* to admit he broke the law, even though he didn't actually break any law, then we give the facts to the Commissariat for Justice and let them decide.

PEOPLE'S COMMISSAR OF THE INTERIOR

I think setting a perjury trap is the way to go.

As one can surmise, this scenario isn't necessarily fiction. Change the names, the setting, the agency, add the Logan Act, and it's a sobering reflection of Barack Obama's Federal

Bureau of Investigation—operating as a sort of quasi–banana republic destroying lives and institutions and driven by the determination to maintain omnipotence—loyal to an administration fueled by egomaniacal impulse and a wanton desire to preserve a Kung Fu death grip on power.

At the highest level of the highest law enforcement agency in America, actual conversations about how to frame a man who had not committed a crime, a decorated and distinguished military three-star general with an unblemished record, were happening not just without fear of reprisal but with the approval and direction of the president of the United States. That it's derivative of the Soviet Union's secret police force should scare the bejesus out of any freedom-loving American.

So, just what *was* Michael Flynn's crime? He helped Donald Trump win the presidency. Also, Obama and his henchman didn't like him from his days as head of the Defense Intelligence Agency. At the end of the day, that's really all it was. Oh, and he called a guy on the phone—a former Russian Ambassador named Sergey Kislyak—which was pretty routine for a guy about to become National Security Advis—No, wait. The crime wasn't the call itself; it's what he said during the call. No, wait. It wasn't what was said during the call; it's that Flynn lied to them about what he said during the call. No, wait. Why was he even talking to FBI about the call?

It was a "sting."

We now know the Communist secret police, err, the FBI framed Michael Flynn.

The FBI concocted an "investigation" to make Flynn commit a crime and then indict him for it.

Without informing the Department of Justice, and without approval from White House Counsel, agents from James Comey's FBI, basically a couple of crooked cops, conducted an "ambush" interview of Flynn under false pretenses and entrapped him. As in that fictional Soviet scenario, the leadership of the FBI plotted the interview right down to the wording, debating whether to get Flynn to lie about that phone call so he could be prosecuted, or get him fired. They went with the former—getting him to "lie."

Later the FBI would extract a false "confession" from Flynn by threatening to destroy his son.

It's surprising they didn't subject him to sleep deprivation, beat him with a sock full of oranges, or pummel his crotch with a steel-tipped whip. It might have been less painful than what they actually did do—spending the next three years working tirelessly to destroy Flynn's life for something they knew he did not do.

Again, we know why it happened—the election of Donald J. Trump as forty-fifth president of the United States. That seminal event derailed the Obama administration's eight-year effort to reshape America into a Marxist utopia. And Flynn? He was the Eliot Ness to Obama's Capone, likely to expose the nefarious behavior of a political machine run rampant. The administration was terrified. It knew Flynn, as the incoming national security advisor, would unravel everything: their relentless efforts to undermine Israel and transfer the balance of power in the Middle East to Iran, "Crossfire Hurricane"—the counterintelligence operation to paint Donald Trump as an asset of Russia, and their subversive attempts to oust Trump from office. Obama's administration was so corrupt that it unleashed the full fury of the federal government on a man who'd committed no crime.

The administration was fully consumed with hatred for the newly elected president but even more afraid its legacy would be lost. So, the FBI was weaponized, and a plan was hatched.

Flynn was going down.

ACT 1

WHO IS MICHAEL FLYNN?

CHAPTER 1

HOODLUM

SOLDIER, COMMANDER, DAD, HUSBAND, SON, BROTHER—Michael Thomas Flynn is many things—not the least of which is "survivor." The depth of who he is goes well beyond the false narrative the establishment media pushed on an ill-informed public for the better part of three years.

For example, watching or reading the establishment media, would anyone have known Flynn had been a lifelong Democrat?

Not likely.

To fully appreciate how shamefully Flynn was victimized by a duplicitous FBI and to fully comprehend the absurdity of painting him as a traitor and some sort of Russian agent, one has to understand who he is and how he rose to such a lofty position from such a modest beginning.

There's no need for a deep dive here into *every* nuance of Flynn's early life. That was well documented by Flynn himself, in a bestselling book he wrote in 2016.[1]

Flynn was born at Fort Meade, Maryland, on Christmas Eve in 1958—oddly apropos it was Christmastime given how he was destined to become an innocent man persecuted and crushed for someone else's iniquities. For zealots offended by the comparison, not to worry, that's where the Jesus allegory ends.

Flynn grew up with eight siblings in Middletown, Rhode Island—a picturesque town of farmland, vineyards, beaches, and wide-open space. It's an idyllic spot nestled smack dab in the middle of Aquidneck Island. With fewer than twenty thousand people living there, Middletown's entire population could fit inside Boston Garden. By his own account,[2] Flynn's life in a tiny Tuckerman Avenue house packed with an eleven-person family wasn't the easiest. It seemed a bit Machiavellian, a "Lord of the Flies" fight for survival, or at the very least, a fight for a good bunk or the last piece of toast at the breakfast table. The skills he learned in that house would serve him well later on.

The first sign that there was something really special—an intangible leadership quality—in Michael Flynn unfolded on a fateful summer day in 1972. The thirteen-year-old was outside with friends over on Bailey Terrace when he spotted a runaway car barreling toward two toddlers. There was a child behind the wheel who'd been playing inside the car and inadvertently released its emergency brake, and now a three-thousand-pound steel behemoth was hurtling down the driveway. Flynn, nimble of foot and quick in thought, assessed the danger, yelled at a friend to grab one kid, while he, like a red-caped hero from planet Krypton, swept in and grabbed the other. He saved the lives of two children—while being one himself. Flynn became a legend that day in Middletown—got his picture on the front page of the paper and everything.[3]

Flynn would be honored a couple of weeks later by the Middletown Town Council and again have his picture in the paper, but his fame was short-lived. Even though Flynn had received accolades as a Little League baseball player and as a straight-A middle school student, by the time he grew into full adolescence, Flynn was a juvenile delinquent. He'd been running amok with equally delinquent friends in the quiet town more known for its farmland and beaches than for its gritty streets—Middletown wasn't exactly Detroit—and Flynn was making quite the impression. As he said himself, he was "one of those nasty tough kids hellbent on breaking rules for the adrenaline rush and hardwired just enough to not care about the consequences."[4] (Insert Judas Priest's "Breaking the Law" here.) But consequences would indeed arrive, and as Flynn would learn the hard way, not even the most fleet can outrun Johnny Law. That's how he wound up in the Sockanosset

School for Boys—a reformatory—or as the OG's might know it, "Socko."

Flynn spent a night in that hellhole—a decrepit abyss of despair built in the late 1800s where an asylum for the incurably insane also stood. But as the nineteenth-century abolitionist Henry Ward Beecher famously said, "Troubles are often the tools by which God fashions us for better things." This one night, and the one year he spent on probation—those troubles—served as the tools by which God would fashion Flynn for better things.

He straightened up to be sure, due in no small part to his strict Irish parents. His father, Charles, was a tough-as-nails ex-military man, a veteran of both World War II and the Korean Conflict, who spent more than two decades in the Army. The family patriarch, who'd risen from bank teller to bank vice president after leaving the military, didn't go easy on his son. Charlie Flynn believed in doing things the right way—set a goal and work hard to achieve it.

Helen Flynn, like her husband, was tough, maybe tougher—she gave birth to nine children. Helen also believed in doing things the right way. She not only believed in hard work, she lived it. Helen earned a college degree *while* raising all those children, oh, and ran for state representative, and later, the United States Senate. So, it's not a far-fetched assumption that there'd be no nurturing of young Michael's poor choices.

He'd punched a one-way ticket to Palookaville, and now the ride was over.

The stint in Sockanosset, the probation, the fallout from Mom and Dad—the divine sledgehammer of redemption hit Flynn like, well, a sledgehammer.

The hoodlum from the hardscrabble home (alliteration alert!) straightened up.

Flynn thrust himself into school, in particular, the varsity football team—the Middletown High School Islanders. Mike, or "Flynnie," as he was known then, had mettle—a doggedness honed from surviving a home with four sisters and four brothers that masked a lean, yet toned, frame more suited to surfer than linebacker—makes sense, surfing was, and is a passion. He made first-team all-division. That Islanders team in 1976 was unstoppable. Flynnie, an ironman who played both offense and defense, was made co-captain, and the team steamrolled to the Class B Super Bowl, where it annihilated Smithfield High School and ended the season as Rhode Island Class B state champions. Today, Mike Flynn, along with the rest of that '76 team, is enshrined in the Middletown High School Athletic Hall of Fame.[5]

Flynn the hoodlum had long since been left behind. Now, the shaggy-haired athlete, surfer dude, and stud who was voted "Best Looking" by the senior class was president of the student body and dating Lori, whom he'd later marry. Flynn was a big man on campus—a guy with the world by the tail and a future so bright he had to wear shades. (Cringy '80s song reference alert!) He graduated Middletown High School in 1977 and was now headed for the University of Rhode Island.

But come fall, Flynn would again meet bad habits and rebellion, and an ROTC instructor who would change his life.

CHAPTER 2

MILITARY MAN

1977 WAS A YEAR FOR CHANGE IN AMERICA. JIMMY CARTER was sworn in as president of the United States of America—ushering in a new era of establishment politics—he pardoned the Vietnam War draft dodgers; removed travel restrictions to paradise destinations Cuba, North Korea, Vietnam, and Cambodia, which was run by Pol Pot, the Marxist-Leninist whose record on human rights falls somewhere between Hitler and Chairman Mao; and proposed the abolition of the Electoral College—oh, and he signed the Torrijos-Carter Treaties, which ultimately ceded the United States' control of the Panama Canal to Panama. Quite the first year. Can't imagine why two years later, with the United States buried under crushing inflation, unemployment, and an energy crisis, Carter would tell Americans they had a crisis of confidence and a "growing doubt about the meaning of our own lives and in the loss of a unity of purpose for our nation." Hmm, who could have been responsible been for that? A president who makes policy decisions that destroy the American way of life and then criticizes Americans for the way they live—not exactly a "Keep America Great" kinda guy.

1977 was also a banner year for disco, KISS, men wearing giant Krugerrands hanging from gold rope chain necklaces, the newly unveiled Apple II personal computer, shiny polyester shirts, mood rings, free love, and, for reasons only the fashion gods themselves know, Earth Shoes—so popular the company went broke later in the year because it couldn't keep up with demand. People packed theaters for George Lucas's *Star Wars,* likely because the groundbreaking science-fiction fantasy provided a welcome respite from a lingering national malaise.

At the University of Rhode Island, *Renaissance,* the school's yearbook, noted, "Our blue jeans and long hair have given way to disco-style clothes and angles haircuts," and pondered, "Should the Union be an outlet for beer and wine? Should the Pub and the Cuproom push alcohol?"[6] These are the kinds of contemplative questions a lot of college kids had then. Life for an eighteen-year-old student was substantially less complicated, as it was for incoming freshman, Mike Flynn.

His life wasn't complicated by classes—he skipped them. Okay, not all of them, but the classes he did attend, Flynn likely never studied for. He shared the same grade point average as the esteemed academic Pinto from *Animal House,* a decidedly less-than-Mensa 1.2.[7] That's essentially two Cs, two Ds, and an F. This was an inauspicious start for a destined-to-be three-star Army general. The good news? He never knew Dean Wormer.

Flynn entered college at an odd time for the country. Under Carter, America was still trying to catch its footing. A whirling dervish of ideologies cast a pall over politics, pop culture, and college campuses. The bicentennial was in the rearview mirror, confidence in Washington wasn't particularly high, the country's economy was abysmal, Watergate and Gerald Ford's pardon of Richard Nixon were still fresh, and it had only been a couple of years since the fall of Saigon and the disastrous end to the Vietnam War. It's not a stretch to say there wasn't a long line of eager, doe-eyed young men outside the military recruiting office. Flynn certainly wasn't. Instead, he dropped out, went surfing, and worked as a lifeguard.

But a fortuitous encounter with a guy on a basketball court changed everything.

Flynn played ball with an instructor from the Reserve Officers Training Corp (ROTC) at URI who saw something in him—maybe the same qualities that led him to saving those two girls from the runaway car when he was thirteen. In the summer of 1978, the instructor told Flynn that if he'd stop screwing around, study, and earn good grades, he'd get him a scholarship.[8]

The nineteen-year-old took the offer and stayed true to his commitment. A seemingly rudderless young man, who preferred surfing to studying, grabbed hold of the opportunity and poured himself both into school and the Army ROTC. Three years after meeting the transformative instructor who believed in him, Flynn earned his Bachelor of Science degree in Management Science from the University of Rhode Island and was honored as an Army ROTC Distinguished Military Graduate. He'd later go on to earn three graduate degrees—an MBA in telecommunications from Golden Gate University in San Francisco, the Master of Military Arts and Sciences from Fort Leavenworth in Kansas, and a Master in National Security and Strategic Studies from the United States Naval War College in his home state of Rhode Island. And to add the bow on top of an already impressive package, Flynn also holds an honorary Doctorate of Law from The Institute of World Politics in Washington, DC.

That's what's known as seriously getting your crap together.

Flynn was commissioned a second lieutenant and entered the Army in 1981 assigned to its Military Intelligence Corp. Flynn's professor of military science—a Special Forces lieutenant colonel—saw that he had an aptitude for intelligence, even more so than for infantry work, so Flynn made a branch assignment request and was accepted.[9]

He went off for intelligence training in exotic Fort Huachuca in the scorching Arizona desert, and Massachusetts's Fort Devens, a quick ten-minute drive from Harvard. Flynn had real proficiency for the military. His first assignment was at Fort Bragg, North Carolina, where he was a paratrooper in the 82nd Airborne Division—a division he would one day command. Over the next thirty-three years, Flynn would earn one promotion after another commanding at the platoon, company, battalion, and brigade levels, and enjoy a distinguished career that could fill a book all its own.

But it was on a day early in his career when the rest of the Army would find out Flynn was no ordinary military man.

It had been just three years since he entered the Army, and Flynn was leading a platoon on the island nation of Grenada as part of Operation Urgent Fury—the American-led invasion that helped usher in democracy there. Grenada had been under communist rule since a revolution four years earlier by the New Jewel Movement, and the military forces of the United States swept in, threw out the Cuban army, and helped slow the influence of communism sweeping through the Caribbean.

On this particular day, the politically oppressed weren't the only ones who needed saving; a couple of soldiers did too. In another life-defining, almost-too-good-to-be-true moment, Flynn was that thirteen-year-old kid again—the one on Bailey Terrace who saved those two other kids from the runaway car. While out checking on his intelligence teams, Flynn found himself on a cliff overlooking the ocean, and there he got word a couple of soldiers were in trouble. In the distance, he spotted the two on a raft. They were caught in a heavy current, clearly panicking and being dragged out to sea. In that moment—as he did in the driveway when he saved those two children—Flynn instinctively knew he had to do something. In a move one part Superman, one part Aquaman, and two parts daredevil French cliff diver Lionel Franc, Flynn—remember, he'd been a lifeguard—launched himself into a forty-foot dive from the cliff, swam out, and rescued the soldiers by pulling them back to a spot where a helicopter could pick them up.

An officer who served with him told *The Washington Post* that act of heroism "established the legend of Michael Flynn."[10]

As the saying goes, heroes get remembered, but legends never die.

Flynn had a way of making people take notice.

After Grenada, he honed his craft in military intelligence across three training assignments and wound up again billeted at Fort Bragg, North Carolina, where over the entirety of his military career, he'd spend nearly sixteen years.

In the early '90s, Flynn found himself back in the Caribbean—once again on assignment helping spread freedom to people ruled by a tyrannical regime—this time in Haiti for Operation Uphold Democracy. Seven months after

Jean-Bertrand Aristide became Haiti's first democratically elected president, he was overthrown in a bloody military coup led by a murderous psychopath named Lieutenant General Raoul Cédras. During his reign, Cédras was responsible for the torture, rape, and murder of thousands of Haitians. The United States spent three years trying to deal with this bottom-feeder through diplomatic avenues to no avail. President Bill Clinton decided the time had come to act, because, as he said in a radio address to the nation, "Their reign of terror, a campaign of murder, rape, and mutilation, gets worse with every passing day."

Flynn was made the chief of joint war plans, and his role—as the title says—was to take part in planning the operation. Even though the operation proved a success by ousting the junta and restoring Aristide, it succeeded despite itself. Flynn saw areas in the operation that would need improvement as the military moved forward. He learned that superior intelligence could make up for deficiencies in other areas, and America's military intelligence was woefully unprepared for when boots hit the ground.

These were valuable lessons Flynn took with him to the next assignment in Fort Polk, Louisiana, where his intelligence career was really about to take off.

CHAPTER 3

INTELLIGENCE GUY

TO MOST CIVILIANS, MILITARY INTELLIGENCE WORK IN THE 1980s might appear a sexy assignment. The United States and the Soviet Union were fighting the Cold War, and our idea of "intelligence" largely mimicked Hollywood's. It was espionage—James Bond and films like Clint Eastwood's *Firefox*—spies operating in the shadows of a foreboding underworld filled with intrigue and danger. But fact and fantasy rarely align in military intelligence, and Flynn was no trench-coated operative.

He was a thinker, as he proved in both Grenada in 1983 and in Haiti in the '90s.

Flynn's aptitude for intelligence earned him a promotion to Senior Observer/Controller for Intelligence—basically, the head of intelligence training—at Fort Polk, home of the Joint

Readiness Training Center. There, he worked alongside more senior officers whose experience would prove invaluable in teaching him the fine art of intelligence and strategic planning for battle. He immersed himself in his work, and it didn't take long for Flynn to determine the military's interrogation policies were in dire need of revamping and that the Army, when it came to its intelligence system, was, to quote Roman Nagel in the film *Ocean's 13*, "analog players in a digital world." It was stuck in a Cold War mindset or, worse, a World War II mindset—believing wars would be won solely with brawn and brute force. Flynn saw there was a new kind of enemy and that it couldn't be defeated with tanks alone. He wanted military intelligence to be more nimble, more technologically advanced, and with less top-down management.

So, he rolled up his sleeves and went to work.

Flynn fast established that the old-school ways of conducting intelligence needed dragging into a more modern approach—a new paradigm. Some of the old guard found this off-putting, but the free-thinking intelligence maverick ushered in protocols for special ops intelligence that broke new ground—primarily in the Middle East. If there was an operation with the word "desert" in its name, Flynn was involved—Desert Shield, Desert Storm, Desert Fox, and Desert Thunder II—through his assignments with the 82nd Airborne, 18th Airborne Corps, and the Joint Special Operations Command (JSOC) at Fort Bragg.

Fort Polk was now in the rearview, and JSOC was the focus—and *its* primary focus was, and is, counterterrorism. As one might surmise, JSOC is a joint command between the Army, Navy, and Air Force, and what happens within the walls of its base complex is about as "hush-hush" as it gets. While he was there, Flynn took the term "*joint* operations" seriously and advocated heavily for more sharing of gathered intelligence. He also dealt with those interrogation policies he deemed in need of change. Flynn came up with inventive new methods of interrogation that were substantial in the United States' counterterrorism efforts during Operation Enduring Freedom and Operation Iraqi Freedom in Afghanistan and Iraq.

To use a well-worn phrase, Flynn thought "outside the box." This guy was a major force in destroying the infrastructure of the insurgency in Iraq—dismantling the networks wreaking havoc throughout the region—largely by using technology in ways that hadn't been used before. It can't be overstated how hugely successful this was in throwing al-Qaida's efforts into disarray. Flynn employed drones to penetrate terror cells, extracted intel from captured cell phones, and located new targets simply by analyzing the intel that his soldiers got after infiltrating a terror group. He was the principal player in special ops intelligence.

Flynn recognized the United States was fighting a different kind of war—more so than even Vietnam—different than those tank battles of the past where we did so well. In

Vietnam, we'd involved ourselves in that country's civil war, but the fight wasn't really with North Vietnam; it was with the Soviet Union—a Cold War proxy fight—good versus evil. Winners and losers. But in Iraq and Afghanistan, the reality was never so clear-cut. No one in the Coalition really knew who among the Iraqis and Afghans was with them. There were so many tribal offshoots, it was no easy task separating the wheat from the chaff. In the end, what was defined as a win? What was a loss? Guerrilla warfare in the Middle East was at odds with any battle we'd ever waged.

Flynn determined that the military's intelligence protocols needed radical transformation if the United States and the Coalition were to succeed in this theater. But, just as important, he determined, the politicians needed a swift kick in the ass. Flynn surmised many of the intelligence failures in Iraq and Afghanistan weren't the result of bad analytics of the collected intel but were policy failures from the top ranks. He believed these failures were the result of policymakers dismissing good information when it conflicted with their accepted narrative.[11]

Sound familiar?

Flynn had no hesitancy to call it as he saw it, privately or publicly. In fact, he co-wrote a blistering essay nakedly revealing what he thought were intelligence failures in Afghanistan, and for reasons no one knows for certain, Flynn allowed a think tank—The Center for a New American Security—to publish it.[12] It's one thing to criticize military intelligence ops in private—running concerns up the flagpole, maintaining chain of command—but opining on its shortcomings in public? That's either career suicide or a power move that elevates your profile and (or) forces change. It's been said there's a fine line between genius and insanity, and whatever the motive for his consistent outspokenness, Flynn looked like a genius. His professional path showed no signs of slowing; in fact, it accelerated at warp speed.

In Iraq and Afghanistan, he made a strong impression where it counted—on General Stanley McChrystal—his mentor—the one who'd seen Flynn's potential and put him in charge of intelligence at JSOC. While Flynn's candor in calling out flawed processes irritated some of his superiors, his ideas were often the cogs that powered the intelligence machine, and he enjoyed a well-earned reputation as a master tactician in Iraq and Afghanistan.

The power players at the Pentagon took note. Flynn directed intelligence at the United States Central Command, the Joint Staff, the International Security Assistance Force-Afghanistan, and the U.S. Forces-Afghanistan. He'd also become the Assistant Director of National Intelligence for Partner Engagement, which was right in Flynn's wheelhouse as he was an advocate of the responsible sharing of intelligence. It may be a rote thing to say, but his star was on the rise.

On July 24, 2012, Obama appointed Flynn the Director of the Defense Intelligence Agency (DIA).

Flynn's reputation could be measured by the enormity of this promotion. He was now the United States military's highest-ranking intelligence officer, in charge of all U.S. worldwide military intelligence gathering, and more than 16,000 people from the Army, Navy, Air Force, Marines, and civilians from the Department of Defense (DOD). The DIA planned and executed intelligence ops during both peacetime and war and gave military intelligence to policymakers, planners at the DOD, the intelligence community, and the ones actually fighting the wars. This new assignment provided fertile ground to do what Flynn had a passion for doing—driving change. But as he would soon learn, while change was certainly needed at DIA, it was not necessarily wanted.

The DIA under Obama had a lot of issues. For one, it couldn't, or wouldn't, recognize China's increasing expansionism and its deadly Marxist-Leninist agenda. This would bite them a couple of years later—after Flynn was fired from DIA (more on that in a minute)—when China's General Secretary Xi Jinping stood next to Obama in the Rose Garden and vowed that he wouldn't militarize the South China Sea, which we know was a lie—China's People's Liberation Army was doing it even as Xi said the words. DIA's second issue, and a vastly enormous one at that—the handling of the Middle East.

Flynn's DIA assignment came about a year after Obama's disastrous decision to pull American troops from Iraq, creating a vacuum in which ISIS grew into a mammoth, unchecked agent of evil. Flynn now had the Herculean task of helping clean up the chaotic mess Obama left behind. "Terror" doesn't begin to describe the soulless, repugnant acts of seemingly godless monsters. ISIS murdered children, raped women, sold people into sexual slavery, and killed homosexuals by throwing them off buildings or stoning them. A Jordanian pilot was tossed into a cage, doused with lighter fluid, and burned alive. People were beheaded. Military action was useless without the right intel, but the DIA Flynn walked into didn't recognize radical Islamic terror. And why would it? Obama himself refused to use the term "Islamic terrorism."

The Middle East had gotten way out of hand, due in no small part to Obama's refusal to treat Islamic terrorists like the inhuman savages they were. The question most people on the right side of the aisle had for Obama was "Whose side are you on?" Of course, the answer came later when he secretly sent pallets of U.S. taxpayer cash (in untraceable foreign currencies) to Iran. Flynn went into the DIA determined to address the intelligence deficiencies ruining the region and emboldening ISIS and would tangle with the administration over its claims that al-Qaida was almost defeated, when it wasn't—which would come to irk his boss, and when the boss is the president of the United States, there's only one way this could end.

Flynn worked to reorganize DIA. Remember the old saying, "You can't make an omelet without breaking a few eggs?" He broke more than a few eggs in the form of disgruntled subordinates who lived the mantra, "But we've always done it this way," and they accused Flynn of being too aggressive in the pursuit of agency reform. They never embraced the stark truth that he was hired to return DIA to a mission of supporting warfighters. Flynn's changes weren't likely to win a popularity contest, especially his desire to incorporate analysts from the office into the field. Why was this a surprise to anyone at DIA? Seriously. Flynn wrote about the idea in that think tank essay—"Select teams of analysts will be empowered to move between field elements, much like journalists, to visit collectors of information at the grassroots level and carry that information back with them to the regional command level." Did no one at an "intelligence" agency know this essay—available to the public—existed?

All of us have been in a job where a new boss comes in and wants to do things their own way. That was Flynn. He was headstrong. He had ideas. He wanted those ideas executed, and he didn't soft-pedal. That didn't go over well, especially with the people who thought his management style was aggressive or combative. Fact is, Flynn was a disruptor—in some industries, that's a good thing, but in a monolithic bureaucracy loaded and bloated with comfortable leadership, not so much.

He was detested.

There were two camps—those with Flynn and those against him. Establishment DIA managers tried cutting at his knees every chance they got. That said, Flynn's critics at the agency were the least of his problems. Obama grew to hate him. Flynn was relentless in his criticism of how the administration handled the Middle East—al-Qaida and ISIS in particular—and Obama's weak-kneed approach to Iran. Flynn's other thorn? A petulant, inexperienced Obama lackey named Ben Rhodes. He was the deputy national security advisor and Obama's sage on foreign policy.

Rhodes was an expert on foreign policy. How couldn't he be? In October 1983 when Flynn was tearing through the island of Grenada with the 82nd Airborne, gathering intelligence, and dismantling a communist coup as a platoon leader during Operation Urgent Fury, Rhodes too was on an island, the Upper East Side of Manhattan—the rough and tumble place where he would hone his intelligence skills—like learning how to read—and discovering first-hand, nothing rivaled the adrenaline rush of receiving a sixty-four pack of Crayola crayons, the one with the built-in sharpener.

He was five.

Rhodes wrote speeches. That's it. That was his background. He was a speechwriter. Though he had absolutely no real-world experience whatsoever in intelligence, nor the military—none, mind you—he was, as a profile in *The*

New York Times Magazine highlighted, "the single most influential voice shaping American foreign policy aside from POTUS himself."[13]

Let that marinate. *"The single most influential voice shaping foreign policy."* A speechwriter. What does that say? It says narrative is more important than truth—spin more important than reality. One would think the person influencing the foreign policy of the most powerful nation on Earth—decisions that would affect millions of people worldwide—should have a professional background better than "Oh, he can spin a good yarn." Not in Obama's sphere. The image—the story—was always everything. That's why Obama got elected in the first place.

When it came to what was happening in the Middle East, Flynn didn't buy into "narrative," and when you're someone like Rhodes, where narrative is everything, that makes for uneasy bedfellows. It's easy crafting theories about Iraq from the comfort of a White House office. Flynn didn't have that luxury. He was actually there—knee-deep in the mire. He saw terrorism first-hand. He didn't read about it in a brief. His analysis was born from experience. Rhodes had none. There was good reason why the two weren't aligned on Iraq, Iran, or quite frankly, any intelligence issue. The rest of Obama's high-level intelligence types were the same—pushing narratives instead of truth. This was 180-degrees counter to Flynn's stated approach, "The fundamental requirement for good intelligence was and is total commitment to the truth."[14] Truth at the Obama White House was relative, merely collateral damage, and soon, Flynn would be too.

The malevolence didn't stop with Obama and Rhodes; it included Flynn's other boss, Director of National Intelligence James Clapper. He too couldn't stand Flynn's refusals to push the administration's narratives.

The animus between Clapper and Flynn went on naked display on April 11, 2013, after a DIA intelligence assessment on North Korea was presented at a public hearing on Capitol Hill. It concluded North Korea had the capability to arm a long-range missile with a nuclear warhead. That afternoon, in a statement, Clapper contradicted the claim. Then he did it again before the Senate Armed Services Committee. Clapper, in full view of C-SPAN cameras, threw DIA's assessment under the bus—"North Korea has not, however, fully developed, tested, or demonstrated the full range of capabilities necessary for a fully armed missile."[15] Then he twisted the knife, "As DIA or others in the intelligence community have similar or differing positions, there can also be varying degrees of confidence in those positions."[16] *"Varying degrees of confidence in those positions."* Imagine having a boss who tells the world he's not confident in your position—a boss who can't say, "I can't speak for other intelligence agencies, but in *our* agency's position, I am confident."

It came down, once again, to narrative. When Obama campaigned to be president, among his promises was the elimination of nuclear weapons. Leading up to that day in April, he had gutted America's missile defense systems—cutting billions from the budgets or killing systems altogether. Obama embraced a Pollyanna vision—a world free of nukes. Flynn didn't live in that world, the one filled with rainbows and unicorns. He lived in the actual world where domination, disorder, and death are the calling cards of despots bent on destroying America by any means necessary—including nuclear weapons.

Flynn's facts were inconvenient truths to Obama, Rhodes, and Clapper—truths to which they turned a blind eye—because those truths didn't fit the narrative—didn't fit the agenda. That's what's known as the politicizing of intelligence. Flynn refused to buy in, and they hated him for it.

Eighteen months after Flynn got the job, Obama and his ilk had had enough. Clapper fired him.

Flynn was allowed to stay on another few months. On April 30, 2014, he announced his retirement from the DIA.

A distinguished three-decade military career was over.

But Flynn's troubles with Obama, Clapper, and other Obama minions weren't. They knew how to hold a grudge, and when the time was right, they'd have their comeuppance.

CHAPTER 4

CITIZEN FLYNN

FLYNN'S FORCED EARLY RETIREMENT FROM DIA INFURIATED him. Why wouldn't it? He was bested by dishonest people who put politics above lives, agenda over truth, and quite frankly, were just plain smug. For an accomplished three-star general accustomed to winning, this stung.

After more than three decades, Flynn found himself asking, "What's next?" Here was the world's foremost expert on military intelligence in a place where he hadn't been in a very, very long time—on the outside. But as he showed throughout the entirety of his life, Flynn wasn't a guy content to sit around. He was a doer, and his next step was to do what he did best—assess, reassess, analyze, and interpret. That's what an intelligence man does. So, Flynn did what he was so good at for thirty-three years: He took stock of the situation and reasoned the next logical step.

He launched the Flynn Intel Group (FIG).

The company was, as you'd expect, an intelligence, cybersecurity, and lobbying firm offering its services to businesses, corporate executives, and government leaders. Flynn's partner in this venture was a man named Bijan Rafiekian, a former member of the board of directors for the Export-Import Bank of the United States who later served on the Trump transition team. He too would be destroyed by Robert Mueller and accused, along with Flynn, of being an agent of Turkey. What is it with these people? Everyone is some sort of foreign agent. (Insert eye roll here.) If you believed Mueller's team, all the people in Trump's circle are agents of KAOS with Bernie Kopell's "Siegfried" pulling the strings. It's become a *Get Smart*–type farce. It'd be comical if it wasn't so pathetic.

A jury later convicted Rafiekian of "conspiracy" and acting as an "unregistered agent of a foreign government," but the judge tossed out the convictions and acquitted him because, as he wrote in his judgment, "There is no substantial evidence that Rafiekian agreed to operate subject to the direction or control of the Turkish government." So, as we've seen time and again, an effort to label someone a "foreign agent" sees an establishment prosecutor become Wile E. Coyote with an ACME bomb blowing up in their face.

Besides FIG, Flynn also took to the public speaking circuit and television commentary. Given the wealth of his knowledge and experience, Flynn was a hot commodity. The muzzle was off, and if he was outspoken in the *public* sector, Flynn was that much more so in the private one.

Flynn wrote a bestselling book, along with Michael Ledeen, a former consultant to the National Security Council, called, *The Field of Fight: How We Can Win the Global War Against Radical Islam and Its Allies*, which was heavily critical of America's inability to confront radical Islamic terrorism head-on. While sometimes disapproving of how administrations dating back to Carter dealt with the Middle East, Flynn teed it up on Obama—"In today's Third World, Obama has shown great sympathy for anti-American revolutionaries… Just as Carter was reluctant to challenge Communist control in the Soviet Union, Cuba, and Nicaragua, so Obama has been reluctant to support domestic opponents of Islamist regimes in Damascus and Tehran."[17] To compare any president to Jimmy Carter in areas of foreign policy, that's as gentle as a steel-toed boot to the testicles.

Flynn proved a pesky thorn in the side of the administration by continually calling out what he saw as major policy failures, not just because they weren't effective, but because they were anti-American—"Obama has done his damnedest to forge alliances with Hugo Chavez, before his death, the Castro brothers, and [the Supreme Leader of Iran] Ali Khamenei."[18]

Flynn viewed America the same way as John Winthrop, one of the original American settlers, as a city upon a hill, the eyes of all people upon us, and knew first-hand Obama didn't also see it that way. Flynn saw an administration cultivating weakness and fear, and let people know that's how he felt. "We have forgotten how to win wars. There is a weakness in our own ability to go in, and from a pure military perspective, and truly crush our enemies," Flynn said at a talk held by The Heritage Foundation to promote his book.[19] "We should not be afraid, we should not fear what our country was built on—a set of Judeo-Christian principles."

Obama devalued the impact of radical Islamic terror simply by refusing to acknowledge it as such. To paraphrase nineteenth-century poet Lord Alfred Douglas, to Obama radical Islamic terror was something that we "dare not speak its name." But to Flynn, it was a global threat that, if not defeated, would substantially change the world as we knew it. "There are cultures around the world, and this is not a racist issue, I couldn't care less if someone is purple polka-dotted, this is about internationally acceptable standards of behavior."[20] He worried about the barbarous behavior of Islamic extremists—their human rights abuses and horrific treatment of women and children, and what the world might look like if it wasn't crushed.

As Flynn became more outspoken—his articulated thoughts more brash and more partisan—many on the left, so deliciously lacking in self-awareness, branded him an extremist. Not only did they dislike his rhetoric on radical Islam, they also believed he was in bed with Russia.

In late 2015, Flynn was invited to speak at a tenth-anniversary gala held by RT, formerly known as Russia Today, a global, English-language television news network funded by the Russian government, which is also broadcast in the United States under the moniker, RT America. The event, held in Moscow, brought together prominent politicians, media executives, and experts in foreign policy from around the world. Flynn certainly qualified, as did Green Party presidential candidate, Dr. Jill Stein, who was also in attendance. The purpose of the conference, beyond recognizing RT's ten years of existence, was to bring those experts together to talk about the geopolitical developments over the decade and to exchange ideas about the challenges facing the world in the foreseeable future. "The gig was to do an interview with [RT correspondent] Sophie Shevardnadze, Flynn would tell *The Washington Post*.[21] "It was an interview in front of the forum, probably 200 people in the audience. My purpose there was I was asked to talk about radical Islam in the Middle East."

Flynn was seated at a table, the same table as Stein, watching the program before dinner was served. Before you could say, "Comrade, I'll have a Stolichnaya and tonic, hold the tonic," the president of Russia, Vladimir Putin himself, sat down. A photograph of the two men at the table later made the rounds through the mainstream media to prove the alliance of Flynn and the evil empire. Like a snowball barreling down a hill, this fairly innocuous photo—rather, the narrative around it—grew larger and larger and larger.

It made for nifty, narrative-affirming copy—"December 10, 2015: Michael Flynn travels to Russia; meets with President Vladimir Putin," declared CBS News.[22] "Former White House national security adviser Mike Flynn accepted an invitation to Moscow in late 2015 to Russian state network RT's 10-year anniversary gala, where *he sat beside President Vladimir Putin*," captioned *The Wall Street Journal*.[23] "Disgraced Trump national security adviser Michael Flynn was paid $45,000 for speech in Moscow at dinner *where he sat beside Putin*," trumpeted *Daily Mail*.[24] And, the pièce de résistance from *Mother Jones*, "The Photo That May Help Unlock the Trump-Russia Scandal."[25]

Scandalous? Yes.

True? Not so much.

Flynn didn't meet with or sit beside Vladimir Putin.

The person who corroborates this? Stein. Speaking on a 2017 podcast, she recounted the night: "If you look closely, if you blow up the picture, you'll see there's a chair between Michael Flynn and Putin, which was occupied by the head of RT. She happened to be introducing Putin at that moment."[26] Stein went into detail telling the host—the co-founding editor of *The Intercept*—Jeremy Scahill what transpired next:

SCAHILL: "And then Putin gets up to give his speech?"

STEIN: "Yup."

SCAHILL: "And then does he return to the table?"

STEIN: "No. Then they walk out. He was basically there to give a speech. This was not some kind of a dinner meeting. Nobody even met anybody. There were, I didn't hear any words exchanged between English speakers and Russians."

SCAHILL: "Did Putin come around the table to say hi to everyone?"

STEIN: "So, I believe it was just before he made his speech, I think. He did a very perfunctory rapid-fire tour around the table. Didn't say a word, just handshake, handshake, handshake, handshake, handshake. That was it. No names exchanged."[27]

Putin and Flynn never even spoke. Interestingly, when Stein was running for president in 2016, no mainstream media outlet mentioned her "meeting" with Putin. None accused her of colluding with Russia. None trotted out an overused photograph showing her at the table. Not a single entity questioned why she'd attended a banquet hosted by a Russia-backed network. Questions like that are reserved for those on the right side of the aisle, or the wrong, depending on perspective.

Regardless of the public, partisan attacks, Flynn was doing well. FIG was doing well. He was in demand as a speaker, and his expertise translated well to business. Flynn sat on the boards and advisory councils or consulted for roughly two dozen companies. He was now well-known throughout business and political circles and certainly familiar to the viewers of the networks on which he appeared, but Flynn's name wasn't yet a household one.

That would change bigly with one fortuitous meeting.

CHAPTER 5

CAMPAIGN WARRIOR

In June 2015, Flynn met Donald J. Trump.

It was brief and informal but made enough of an impression that someone on the Trump campaign staff called Flynn a couple of months later and asked if he'd be interested in meeting. Trump had announced his candidacy for president just before they'd met in June and wanted an advisor with Flynn's credentials. But Trump wasn't the only GOP candidate interested in him. There'd ultimately be seventeen candidates, and they all needed the experienced voice of a guy who'd been in the trenches of intelligence and knew more than a thing or two about national security interests. Besides Trump—Senator Ted Cruz, Governor Scott Walker of Wisconsin, Dr. Ben Carson, and Carly Fiorina all contacted Flynn. He would advise a couple of them, but it was the boorish billionaire with the itchy Twitter finger with whom Flynn truly hit it off. "I was very impressed. Very serious guy. Good listener. Asked really good questions," Flynn would tell *The Washington Post.*[28] When asked what specifically stood out about Trump during their meeting, Flynn was clear, "I think his view of the world and his view of where America was, and where it needed to be. I got the impression this was not a guy who was worried about Donald Trump, but a guy worried about the country. I don't think people can BS me that easily, and I was sort of looking for that. I found him to be in line with what I believed."

In February 2016, it was official—Flynn began serving as an adviser to the Trump presidential campaign.

Like his candidate, Flynn left subtlety by the wayside. On the campaign trail, he was a Dylan Thomas poem come to life. And if there was anyone who did not go quietly into that good night, it was Michael Flynn. With the piss and vinegar of an opinionated general who'd been stifled for too long, Flynn took his rhetoric, shot it with steroids, and fired up Trump's populist base.

He found an eager audience.

Flynn impressed Trump and the campaign to such a degree that once Trump locked up the nomination, the campaign considered and vetted Flynn as a potential running mate. As we know, they went with Indiana Governor Mike Pence instead.

By the time the campaign rolled into Cleveland in July 2016, Trump's momentum was barreling like a locomotive, and Flynn rode it to the then-defining moment of his post-military life—a blistering twenty-six-minute speech at the Republican National Convention. He unleashed everything—all the percolating frustration, anger, and irritation of the Obama years. "Tonight, Americans stand as one with strength and confidence to overcome the last eight years of the Obama-Clinton failures such as bumbling indecisiveness, willful ignorance, and total incompetence that has challenged the very heart and soul of every American, and single-handedly brought continued mayhem, murder, and destruction into our neighborhoods and onto the world's streets."

The gnawing grudge with Obama now had a platform, unfiltered and nakedly displayed for the world to see. "A Commander-in-Chief does not draw 'red-lines' and then retreat. America does not back down from anyone or anything." The crowd began to chant—USA! USA! USA! "You got it right, baby. Get fired up! This is about our country! We are tired of Obama's empty speeches and his misguided rhetoric!" Flynn was rolling. "This has caused the world to have no respect for America's word nor does it fear our might. Let me be clear, coddling and displays of empathy toward terrorists is not a strategy for defeating these murderers as Obama and Hillary Clinton would like us to believe."

Flynn was picking Obama apart—his handling of the Middle East, the lack of proper action against ISIS, the economy, and the "apology" tour—"We do not need a weak, spineless President who is more concerned about issuing apologies than in protecting Americans."

The animus flowed from every pore.

Then came the thundering climax, after which everyone in America would know Flynn's name—he hit Hillary Clinton's email scandal. "We do not need a reckless president who believes she is above the law!" The nearly five thousand delegates and alternate delegates in the arena, now worked into a fervor, seized the line and the moment and began chanting, "Lock her up! Lock her up! Lock her up!" Flynn, caught in the moment too, went with it. "Lock her up, that's right. Yes, that's right! Lock her up! I use the hashtag 'Never Hillary!' I have called on Hillary Clinton to drop out of the race because she put our nation's security at extremely high risk with her careless use of a private email server. [Crowd again chants, "Lock her up!"] "Lock her up. Lock her up. Damn right! You're exactly right. You know why we're saying that?! We're saying that because if I—a guy who knows this business—if I did a tenth of what she did, I would be in jail today!" That was gasoline on a still-smoldering fire. The crowd continued its chant, and Flynn drove it home, "So, Crooked Hillary Clinton, leave this race now!"

That left a mark.

Flynn reportedly regretted getting caught up in the moment and the "lock her up" elements of his speech.[29] The optics were especially bad when he later encountered his own legal troubles. This was also a severe left-turn on a career path marked with a simmering intensity veiled by steely-eyed calm. Retired generals typically toe the line—publicly supporting the commander-in-chief or saying nothing at all. Flynn deviated wildly from that road well-traveled and charted his own—one that would take him to places he never saw on the map.

But in this moment—this moment defined the campaign. In so many ways, Flynn personified the things for which Trump stood—the ideologies of making America great again.

On November 8, 2016, Trump was elected president of the United States—forty-eight hours later he'd be meeting with Obama for the first, and only, time in the Oval Office. Little could Flynn have known that he'd gotten so far under Obama's skin, that among the issues the most powerful man in the world felt compelled to discuss with his successor was Michael Flynn. Obama—his signature cool demeanor masking a certain indignance—attempted to torpedo any opportunity Flynn might have in the new administration. He brought up Flynn's incendiary words about radical Islamic terror, the troubles he'd had at DIA, and that pesky RT gala, you know, the one where Flynn "sat next to Putin." Obama warned Trump not to hire Flynn.

Eight days later, Trump named Flynn national security adviser.

CHAPTER 6

WELP, THAT DIDN'T TAKE LONG

FLYNN'S TENURE AS NATIONAL SECURITY ADVISOR LASTED twenty-four days. He'd been on the job for just four days when a couple of crooked cops—agents of James Comey's FBI—executed a perjury trap to ensnare him. It led to the false accusation that Flynn lied to investigators and would unleash the hounds of legal hell that, as this manuscript went to press, Flynn was still fighting.

During the transitional period before Trump took office, Flynn made a call to then-Russian ambassador to the United States, Sergey Kislyak. That sort of call—to an ambassador of a foreign country—is a routine part of establishing working relationships in a position like Flynn's. It's only problematic when an outgoing administration sets someone up for a fall and twists the narrative.

Flynn was accused of misleading Pence and others in the White House about what was discussed during this call with Kislyak—that he asked Russia not to retaliate for the sanctions levied against it by the Obama administration as Obama's term came to a close.

Three years later, when unsealed documents proved Flynn had been set up by the FBI, Pence told reporters, "I'm inclined, more than ever, to believe that what he communicated to me during the transition leading to our inauguration, that was unintentional and not—and that he was not attempting to misrepresent facts."[30]

But in February 2017, no one publicly expressed that kind of support for the beleaguered national security advisor. Flynn was caught in a tightly squeezed vise and had little choice but to agree to Trump's request that he resign. So, on February 13, Flynn did just that.

In his resignation letter, Flynn related that calls like the one he had with Kislyak are commonplace for anyone in his position. Then, he fell on his sword. "In the course of my duties as the incoming national security advisor, I held numerous phone calls with foreign counterparts, ministers, and ambassadors. These calls were to facilitate a smooth transition and begin to build the necessary relationships between the President, his advisors and foreign leaders. Such calls are standard practice in any transition of this magnitude," Flynn explained. "Unfortunately, because of the fast pace of events, I inadvertently briefed the Vice President-Elect and others with incomplete information regarding my phone calls with the Russian ambassador. Have sincerely apologized to the President and the Vice President, and they have accepted my apology."

For anyone who'd been following Trump's rise to power, it was painfully apparent the Deep State was hunting for ways to destroy him, and they'd bagged their first prey.

Flynn had to be eliminated. He knew where the bodies were buried, so to speak. As national security advisor, he'd uncover the Obama administration's criminal efforts to falsely link Trump to Russia, and they couldn't let that happen. Flynn also held firm to the belief that Obama was sympathetic to radical Islamic terrorists and that he worked ceaselessly to skew the balance of power in the Middle East toward Iran. Obama and his minions knew Flynn was in a position to reveal everything they'd done for Iran's leader, Ali Khamenei—and ultimately, Iranian terrorist, General Qasem Soleimani—and would likely undo it all.

ACT 2

SHADY STUFF THEY KNEW FLYNN WOULD UNCOVER

CHAPTER 7

THE IRAN NUCLEAR DEAL

IRAN SALIVATES AT THE IDEA OF BEING A NUCLEAR SUPERPOWER, and with them, there's no doctrine of mutually assured destruction. The MAD doctrine is based on the idea that if two countries have the capabilities to annihilate one another, neither will act. But the idea that Khamenei would hesitate to push the button if given the chance is a supremely misguided one.

It's also laughable to assume Iran acts alone.

For decades Iran has worked to build its nuclear program with the help of Russia—who builds the power plants—and North Korea. The Pyongyang-Tehran union is an alliance of evil dating back at least three decades—and the two don't even try to hide their unholy bond.

In 2015, even as the United States, along with the European Union, China, France, Russia, the United Kingdom, and Germany, was negotiating the Joint Comprehensive Plan of Action (JCPOA)—commonly known as the "Iran Nuclear Deal"—to stem Iran's development of nukes, a contingent of experts in ballistic missiles, guidance systems, and nuclear warheads from North Korea was visiting a military site near Tehran.[1] On April 2, Obama announced the framework for the historic deal proclaiming it would "prevent it (Iran) from obtaining a nuclear weapon." In a Rose Garden briefing, the great orator spoke of international inspectors having "unprecedented" access to Iranian nuclear facilities and the supply chain supporting them. "With this deal, Iran will face more inspections than any other country in the world," he promised.

Obama warned that inspections could happen "anywhere, anytime." But in the end, the actual agreement wasn't close to that; instead it gave Iran twenty-four days' notice of an inspection. Obama also cut secret side deals that no one—not even in his own administration—saw.[2] One deal was so terrifically ludicrous it defied comprehension to anyone other than the galactically stupid. It allowed Iran to use *its own* inspectors to investigate suspected nuclear weapons facilities.

One had to wonder, whose side was Obama on?

As history would show, the Iran Nuclear Deal didn't require Iran to dismantle its nuclear program, nor did it force them to stop enriching uranium.

Nevertheless, the White House carried on with its dog and pony show. Obama waxed poetic on granting Iran sanctions relief if they took steps to adhere to the agreement but warned if they violated the deal, "sanctions can be snapped back into place." Pretty tough talk for a guy who would later orchestrate his own deal with Iran that would secure the release of men being held prisoner there—men he tried to sell to the American public as Iranian-American "businessmen"—who were actually working to help Iranian arms traders get vital materials for its nuclear and ballistic missile programs.[3]

Two years earlier, in 2013, Obama entered into an interim agreement with Iran that he claimed froze Iran's nuclear program. At the time, they had enough low-enriched uranium to build anywhere from a single nuclear weapon to, at the most, three. But, by the time the final agreement was signed in 2015, Obama stood on the State Floor of the White House and proclaimed, "Iran currently has a stockpile that could produce up to ten nuclear weapons." Interesting. Riddle me this, Batman—if Iran's nuclear program had been frozen for two years, then how could it go from the capability of building only one to three nukes to then being equipped to build ten? As the United States Senate Republican Policy Committee noted at the time, "A five-fold increase in capability is hardly a nuclear program that is frozen."

When Flynn was the senior intelligence officer at United States Central Command, he knew Iran was developing its nuclear weapons program at a steady clip. He also knew North Korea was helping them—and that Iran was operating nuclear weapons sites in Syria with North Korean help. But the more Flynn learned about the Iran/North Korea connection, and how they were able to keep their sites hidden, the angrier he became with what he called, "beyond being an intelligence failure."[4]

The connection with North Korea wasn't the only villainous partnership in which Iran was engaged—it was a longtime supporter of al-Qaida. Terrorism and Iran are so inextricably linked, and have been for so long, it's no revelation that in 1984 the State Department designated the country a "state sponsor of terror." They're one of just four countries on that list. The others? Syria, Sudan, and—yep—North Korea.

And this is the country Obama wanted us to believe would have honor in its dealings? That it would play nicely with us in the sandbox? If you bought into that and believed Iran would simply sign an agreement and that its nuclear weapons development would go quietly into that good night, then I've got a plate of healthy, high-quality gas station sushi I'd like to sell you.

Flynn knew Iran would never play according to the rules of any "deal"—that their war with America was lock, stock, and two smoking barrels perpetually tied to militant Islamic fundamentalism. They'd never abdicate their beliefs for any "deal." And their beliefs included one day nuking the West from here to kingdom come. At the time Obama was announcing this deal, Iran's execution rate was the highest per capita anywhere in the world. When Flynn and other military brass told George W. Bush and later Obama that American troops were encountering Iranians on the battlefields in both Iraq and Afghanistan, in the hopes either president would authorize action against them, neither wanted to hear it.[5]

In that Rose Garden briefing, Obama sold the Iran Nuclear Deal: "Remember, I have always insisted that I will do what is necessary to prevent Iran from acquiring a nuclear weapon, and I will. But I also know that a diplomatic solution is the best way to get this done and offers a more comprehensive and lasting solution. It is our best option, by far."

If you can't beat them with military might, beat them with…conversation?

Obama's nifty wordplay was likely crafted by Deputy National Security Advisor Ben Rhodes—the speechwriter. He witnessed much of the labored relationship between the United States and Iran—after all, in 1979, when Iranian militants took fifty-two Americans hostage and held them for 444 days inside the American Embassy in Tehran, Rhodes was almost two years old.

He was the master of crafting narratives to manipulate masses, and Rhodes wasn't stupid. He knew to get anyone to buy into this farcical Iran deal, he'd have to pull some next-level *Wag the Dog*–type spin from his bag of political tricks.

Rhodes set up a "war room" to orchestrate the campaign—and began the work of swaying the public to support this deal. He worked gullible "journalists" to spread the message, even admitting to *The New York Times*[6] he considered those journalists obtuse, easy marks, and easily manipulated—an "echo chamber" that would push the public toward buying the narrative—a narrative Rhodes all but admitted was a contrivance. "The average reporter we talk to is 27 years old, and their only reporting experience consists of being around political campaigns," he said. "They literally know nothing."[7] Marc Thiessen at *The Washington Post* put it this way: "When it comes to the Iran nuclear deal, the Obama administration increasingly appears to have been a bottomless pit of deception."[8]

Almost everything they said about this Iran deal was a lie.

Reporters were either too lazy, too stupid, too inexperienced, or too enamored with Obama to know or suspect otherwise.

Rhodes himself admitted as much in that revealing *New York Times Magazine* interview—acknowledging he pushed a misleading timeline about when the administration actually started negotiations with Iran because he knew inexperienced reporters would believe it.[9]

The administration wanted the public to believe they'd begun talks with Iran in 2013 after Hassan Rouhani was elected president—a guy viewed by some as more favorable to American interests. That was a lie—on two fronts. Not only was Rouhani not that interested in American interests, the negotiations did NOT start with him—they started under Mahmoud Ahmadinejad, Rouhani's predecessor. As Iran's president, Ahmadinejad, who was both vile and evil (requisite traits for Iran's leaders), held no respect for basic human rights and once said Israel should be wiped off the face of the earth. He was a fan favorite of militant Islamic extremists.

This was the guy Obama first began doing business with—not Rouhani.

Ironically—or not—it was Obama who came to Ahmadinejad and Khamenei's rescue when the two were nearly overthrown. In 2009 the Iranian Green Movement exploded—many of us know it as "Persian Spring"—and millions of Iranians took to the streets protesting their oppressive leadership and calling for Ahmadinejad's removal from power. At the time, Flynn was the senior intelligence officer in Afghanistan for the International Security Assistance Force—just across the border. He noted that the protesting Iranians were desperate for the United States to help, not with military action, but to openly say we stood with them. The leaders of the movement asked Obama to back them up, but he wouldn't. What they didn't know, according to Flynn,[10] was that Obama had a secret outreach to Khamenei through Oman, and that's why Obama stayed silent.

Wow. What more can one say?

The president of the United States of America prioritized a relationship with terrorists over the interests of people seeking freedom.

Wow.

CHAPTER 8

SECRET SIDE DEALS AND PALLETS OF CASH IN THE DEAD OF NIGHT

The arrangement with Khamenei wasn't the only side deal Obama had with Iran. During the negotiations for the nuclear deal, he failed to mention quite a few others.

The level of deceit reached stratospheric heights not seen since…well, ever.

The litany of secret "deals" is long.

There was the "roadmap" agreement between Iran and the International Atomic Energy Agency (IAEA)—that would lift sanctions if Iran committed to providing IAEA with explanations for the "possible military dimensions," or the suspicions that Iran previously conducted a military nuclear program. The problem with this agreement—besides that Tehran, to this day, refuses to cooperate with IAEA—is that no United States official other than Obama knew anything about it. The agreement was stumbled upon by chance by two members of Congress in a meeting with members of IAEA.[11]

The Obama administration secretly helped Iran recover nearly $6 billion in sanctioned assets after it had promised Congress that Iran wouldn't have access to the American financial system. Then they lied to Congress about their actions. This deal was revealed in 2018 when the Senate Permanent Subcommittee on Investigations released the findings of its investigation into the deal in a report called *The Senate Review of U.S. Treasury Department's License to Convert Iranian Assets Using the U.S. Financial System.*

The Obama administration secretly flew $400 million of American taxpayer cash, literal cash money, into Iran. The cash—converted to untraceable foreign currencies like Euros and Swiss francs—was stacked onto wooden pallets and flown into the country on an unmarked cargo plane. One has to figure cash is substantially easier to covertly funnel into the coffers of terrorists. You can't just write a check made out to General Qasem Soleimani with "For Terrorism" on the memo line.

As Trump's Secretary of State Mike Pompeo once said, the only thing Obama's shady deals accomplished was the funding of terror in the region.

The secret transfer of cash was the first installment of a $1.7 billion settlement with Iran over a failed arms deal in 1979. The United States sold them arms but never delivered because of the Iranian revolution. They'd been legally wrangling ever since.

But the questionable cash delivery was so much more than just a payment to satisfy a legal judgment. The money arrived the same day Iran released a handful of Americans being held hostage—so, boiled down to the basics, Obama paid a ransom to one of the largest state sponsors of terror in the world. Clearly, he never got the memo that the United States doesn't negotiate with terrorists—or he just didn't care.

It didn't end there. Over the next few weeks, the administration made two more secret cash shipments to Iran—another $1.3 billion stacked on wooden pallets flown on unmarked cargo planes through Geneva.

Trump would ultimately put an end to all this by pulling the United States from the deal in 2018, reimposing sanctions on Iran, and vaporizing General Soleimani with an airstrike.

Tehran is likely back with its old friend North Korea continuing its subversive development of nuclear weapons. A report by the Foundation for Defense of Democracies shows since the start of the nuclear deal and through 2018, Iran fired twenty-three ballistic missiles, with four or five of them "nuclear capable."[12] And, not incidentally, in January 2020, Iran announced it would no longer abide by the deal—as if it ever had.

Flynn wanted to annihilate radical Islamic terrorists—Obama made deals with them.

Now you know why Obama hated Michael Flynn.

CHAPTER 9

CROSSFIRE HURRICANE (HINT: IT AIN'T JUMPIN' JACK FLASH)

FOR THE BETTER PART OF THREE YEARS, OBAMA-ADMINISTRATION Democrats schemed furiously to prove Donald Trump was an asset of Russia and that his election victory resulted from a coordinated effort by the Russian government to interfere with the American electoral process. They allege Russia hacked DNC computers and also launched a misinformation campaign through ads on Facebook, Twitter,

Instagram, and YouTube—that the 63 million Americans who voted for Donald Trump did so because they saw propagandized social media posts.

The people who believe this scenario likely believe the murders of four Americans at the American embassy in Benghazi in 2012 were the result of a YouTube video. It's as though, somewhere hidden in Siberia's Mount Belukha, Vladimir Putin sits in his secret lair, dressed in a light gray Mandarin-collared suit with Frau Farbissina at his side, laughing maniacally—"muahahahahaha, muahahahahaha"—at how he manipulated America with his diabolical, evil plan.

This sophomoric plot was the contrivance of vengeful, power-hungry Obama hires who wielded it like a sword in the slightest hope it would invalidate Trump's victory. Though it's been officially and formally debunked that Trump ever colluded with Russia, plenty of rubes hold fast to the assertion.

How does Flynn factor into this? The plot to entrap him was a small yet vital cog in the machine—powered by the FBI and fueled by Obama—working to destroy Trump's presidency. That part of the administration's illegal operation would become known as "Obamagate."

The push for an investigation into the Trump campaign and its alleged cooperation with Russia began long before the election—back in 2015—though the "official" investigation dubbed Crossfire Hurricane would begin the following year. "Crossfire Hurricane" comes from the first line of the Rolling

Stones classic "Jumpin' Jack Flash"— "I was born in a crossfire hurricane…" According to Stones guitarist and co-songwriter, Keith Richards, as he wrote in his autobiography, the line refers to his being born during World War II in the midst of a German air raid near London. Just what exactly the FBI suits who named the operation were trying to imply with the reference…who knows? Although *The New York Times* called it "an apt prediction of a political storm that continues to tear shingles off the bureau."[13]

It's not an overstatement that Crossfire Hurricane was the most corrupt operation in the history of American politics—an operation designed to subvert the results of a presidential election, to paint the lawfully elected president as a Russian agent, that Trump conspired with another country to steal an election in the runup to Election Day. Think about the enormity of that accusation.

As mentioned earlier, Watergate is high school hijinks compared to Crossfire Hurricane.

What we now know is it wasn't Trump trying to steal the election, it was Barack Obama…for Hillary Clinton. To do it, he went to his roots—good old-fashioned Chicago-style politics. Shady. Dirty. Underhanded. Lawless.

Obama mobilized and focused the full might of the federal government on destroying Trump and anyone associated with him. It was naked in its vulgarity and single-minded of purpose—to guarantee the election of Hillary Clinton as president.

Illegal wiretaps, perjury traps, manufactured evidence, weaponizing the FBI—Obama and his acolytes demonstrated such a flagrant disregard for the rule of law, the Constitution, and American citizens' legal rights that, in the irony of all ironies, he behaved as though he was president of…Russia.

This was a coordinated criminal enterprise on a grand scale. If he hadn't been president of the United States, Obama would likely be in prison for violating the RICO Act…or treason. Fortunately for him, he had a "D" next to his name when he was president, whereas Nixon had an "R." Meaning? Nixon was forced from office in disgrace. Obama left with a $65 million book deal.

The sordid story of Crossfire Hurricane and the FBI's framing of innocent people starts in 2016. It was prompted by a tip to the feds from Alexander Downer—the former foreign minister of Australia—that an advisor to the Trump campaign named George Papadopoulos was allegedly boasting over cocktails that the Russians had dirt on Hillary Clinton with thousands of her emails.

That's when an FBI agent named Peter Strzok—who detested Trump—filed official paperwork to secure a Foreign Agent Registration Act (FARA) investigation, without listing any legitimate reasons to justify such an investigation, and then approved it himself. Although it was Bill Priestap, the

FBI's chief of counterintelligence, who made the ultimate decision to launch the investigation. It's incomprehensible that the most powerful law enforcement agency in the United States of America could launch an enterprise based on the political biases of corrupt cops—men like Strzok who'd sent text messages to his mistress, an FBI lawyer, saying that Trump was a "douche" whom they would stop from becoming president—but it did.

As the next two years would reveal, Strzok's actions during the operation were sociopathic. He's displayed no remorse or concern for his Soviet-era tactics that destroyed the life, liberty, and pursuit of happiness of every innocent person associated with Trump, including Flynn—just so he could orchestrate a Clinton victory and then, after she lost, destroy the presidency.

Volumes of pages have been written detailing every Crossfire Hurricane player, criminal act, phone call, meeting, and timeline. Rather than deconstruct it all here, we'll stick with the main bullet points. They're enough to illustrate the Deep State's deplorable attempts at a coup and ultimately a sham impeachment, which would later explode in their collective faces.

The sole focus of the enterprise was to color Trump and his top campaign staffers as Russian operatives—and to help Hillary Clinton get elected president of the United States, although the FBI won't admit to the latter. The idea to push the Russia narrative originated with Clinton. She wanted to deflect attention from the FBI's investigation into her use of a private email server when she was secretary of state.

To justify their "investigation," the FBI, led by Director James Comey, relied on information found in a dossier commissioned and paid for by the law firm representing Clinton's presidential campaign, and the Democratic National Committee. They hired Fusion GPS, a private intelligence and research company, to do opposition research, and Fusion contracted a Trump-hating, ex-agent of Britain's MI6 named Christopher Steele to gather the intel.

This dossier, now known as the Steele Dossier, portrayed Trump as a Russian agent and was chock-full of sketchy, unverified information—so contrived, it read as though it were compiled by a sleazy 1940s noir detective. The dossier was so lacking in any kind of corroborated legitimacy that no major news organization would touch it—until BuzzFeed published it, although BuzzFeed's "journalists" aren't exactly Edward R. Murrow.

The FBI determined Steele was talking to reporters about the dossier and ended its "official" relationship with him. However, a Department of Justice official named Bruce Ohr, whose wife worked for Fusion GPS, continued to meet with Steele and fed the information from those meetings to the FBI.

The bureau used the dossier to keep its investigation alive even after it knew the information, or misinformation, in it was planted with Steele in part by Sergei Millian—a

Belarusian-born American businessman with connections to the Russian government—and was spurious at best. So myopic was the agency's anti-Trump agenda that it kept all of its doubts about the dossier from everyone—DOJ lawyers, judges, and the public.

What's worse is the primary subsource for the dossier was a suspected Russian spy who the FBI believed was a "threat to national security." They'd investigated him for two years, from 2009 through 2011. The FBI knew this when Crossfire Hurricane began yet it still used the dossier information to secure warrants for electronic surveillance of Trump staffers. (More on that later.)

The question here is, if the Russians were planting information to *hurt* Trump, then how could they be "colluding" with him to *help* him? Clearly, logic doesn't matter when it opposes the service of a pre-determined narrative.

FBI operatives tapped phones, text messages, and emails. They used an intelligence briefing they gave to Trump when he was a candidate—just two weeks after launching Crossfire Hurricane—as a cover to spy on both Trump and Flynn. Agents pretended they were there to give a "defensive briefing" when they were actually noting any mentions Flynn or Trump made of Russia.

Agents falsified court papers and lied to judges. The behavior was so egregious that in 2019, the DOJ's Inspector General, Michael Horowitz, determined the FBI violated its own rules by knowingly omitting evidence and lying more than a dozen times when obtaining the warrants permitting them to spy.[14] He publicly spanked the agency in a blistering report for failing to disclose the evidence it had disproving the Steele Dossier.

Of course, the FBI couldn't disclose that evidence, nor could it disavow the dossier—it's what they used to get the warrants. Think about that. For the first time in history, the FBI used salacious information paid for by one presidential candidate to spy on the campaign of another presidential candidate. As then-White House Press Secretary Sarah Huckabee Sanders tweeted, "The real Russia scandal? Clinton campaign paid for the fake Russia dossier, then lied about it and covered it up."

The intent was to derail Trump's election chances or to pocket a trump card (pun definitely intended) they'd play to wreck his presidency should he win. When Trump did win, about a month after he took office, *The New York Times* published an article with the headline, "Trump Campaign Aides Had Repeated Contacts with Russian Intelligence."[15] Great headline. Great step toward sullying the presidency. Too bad for them, the story wasn't true. Three and a half months later, when Comey appeared before the Senate Intelligence Committee, Arkansas senator Tom Cotton asked specifically about the *Times* article: "Would it be fair to characterize that story as almost entirely wrong?" Comey's answer? "Yes."

ACT 3

SLAUGHTER OF THE INNOCENT

CHAPTER 10

CARTER PAGE

Crossfire Hurricane had the FBI initially targeting four people in the Trump campaign—the two hired as foreign policy advisors, Carter Page and George Papadopoulos; campaign manager Paul Manafort; and Flynn. The FBI had them in their sights for the sole reason that at some point or another, they'd each had contact with Russians—which wasn't unusual given the line of work they were in.

Page was a retired Naval intelligence officer with an MBA and a PhD who became a successful investment banker and ran the energy and power group at Merrill Lynch before leaving to start his own energy investment firm. He scouted business opportunities in oil-rich Russia while he was working for Merrill Lynch, and he lived in Moscow for a while in the mid-2000s.[1]

So, as far as the FBI was concerned, Page just had to be an agent of Russia.

He was actually working for the CIA as an "operational contact."

This is not an insignificant fact—a fact the FBI knew but ignored.

An unscrupulous FBI lawyer named Kevin Clinesmith, who was wildly anti-Trump, falsified an email from the CIA to the FBI. He informed them that Page had helped with investigations involving Russia. Clinesmith abhorred Trump to such a degree and was so hellbent and determined to put Page under surveillance that he doctored an official document to say Page had *not* worked with the CIA. He did it to justify the FBI's spying on Page so the secretive Foreign Intelligence Surveillance Court would sign off on renewing the warrant under the Foreign Intelligence Surveillance Act (FISA)—which it did.

The FISA court exists to decide government requests for electronic surveillance—wiretaps and the like—to monitor people suspected of being spies or terrorists. Surely had the court known Page wasn't a Russian spy but instead had worked with the CIA to help root out Russian spies, it would not have allowed the FBI to spy on him.

More than likely, the court would have also wanted to know that the evidence upon which the FBI's investigation was based was paid for by the Clinton campaign. But it didn't.

Now armed with their warrant, the FBI monitored Page's communications—his telephones, email, text messages, and the people with whom he'd communicated—for almost a year.

Inspector General Horowitz's investigation determined the FBI never had any legitimate evidence against Page before it began investigating him. Attorney General William Barr would later assign United States Attorney John Durham the task of reviewing the origins of the FBI's Russia investigation, which didn't bode well for Clinesmith. In the first of the convictions resulting from Durham's investigation, Clinesmith got his due. In 2020, he pleaded guilty to doctoring documents. Former Deputy Attorney General Sally Yates told the Senate Judiciary Committee that had she known of the false information Clinesmith included in the FISA warrant application, she wouldn't have signed it.

Sure.

The same woman who helped take down Flynn.

That's a nifty "coulda shoulda woulda," but the damage was done. Page, who'd done nothing wrong, had been relentlessly branded a Russian agent. In fact, the Steele Dossier claimed he was a go-between messenger for Trump and Putin. Senate Minority Leader Harry Reid, the Clinton campaign, and unnamed intelligence sources accused Page of engaging in conversations—while on a visit to Moscow—with officials from the Russian government about the possibility of Trump lifting economic sanctions if he became president. Page called the allegations "complete garbage."[2]

On September 26, 2016, he decided he'd had enough and resigned from the Trump campaign.

Page later sued the DNC and Perkins Coie—the law firm representing the Clinton campaign—for defamation over their use of the Steele Dossier. His lawyers made clear in their filing it was the dossier that led the FBI to unlawfully spy on him—"The defendants are private actors who used false information, misrepresentations and other misconduct to direct the power of international intelligence apparatus and the media industry against a private individual."

But Page wasn't the only private individual they'd ruin.

CHAPTER 11

GEORGE PAPADOPOULOS

IF THERE WERE EVER A PERSON WHO PERSONIFIED THE WORD "wunderkind," George Papadopoulos was it. Before he'd even turned thirty, Papadopoulos was named one of Trump's foreign policy advisors for his 2016 presidential campaign. As the son of Greek immigrants, to grow up to become an advisor to the future president of the United States was probably not something he could have foreseen—not as a kid coming of age near Chicago, not as an undergraduate student at DePaul, and not as a graduate student in London. He also could not have foreseen how that very accomplishment would put him in the gunsights of the FBI.

Like Flynn, Papadopoulos would also be ensnared in an FBI perjury trap.

As we've seen, anyone associated with Trump was prey for the hunt. The FBI sought to destroy every important player in the campaign and, later, the administration, and stopped at nothing to smear each of them as a Russian spy—including his newest advisor. Somehow Papadopoulos was the key master to the gateway of proof—proof that Trump and Putin were comfortable bedfellows.

Truth be told, Papadopoulos had never been to Russia, had no colleagues in Russia, and never worked with anyone from Russia. Yet somehow this twenty-something, barely-out-of-school former researcher at a neoconservative think tank was the key component to toppling a presidency? The absurdity of that notion—that somehow this political tenderfoot was the vital piece to proving Trump was a Russian asset—rivals the notion that Jeffrey Epstein committed suicide.

Papadopoulos wanted to change the world. When he was a student at University College London, he developed a passion for security and geopolitical issues. After graduating with a master's degree in security studies, Papadopoulos began a tireless, oft-frustrating campaign to land a job with a think tank or research institute. As he recounted in the book he wrote about being a target of the FBI, after scores of rejections, Papadopoulos considered enrolling in law school but changed his mind after a random encounter with a lawyer who talked him out of it.[3] He landed a gig with the Hudson Institute think tank, where he impressed his bosses by initiating and building a project fostering an energy alliance between Israel, Greece, and Cyprus with regard to gas found offshore there.

The guy was ambitious. He had swagger and a penchant for self-promotion some found oft-putting—and still do. But it served Papadopoulos well. He knew what he wanted and worked at getting it. When Trump announced he'd be running for president in 2015, Papadopoulos reached out to his campaign manager, Corey Lewandowski, with the hope he'd hire him, but the campaign wasn't yet bringing anyone aboard. The two stayed in touch, which helped down the road, but meantime, after leaving the Hudson Institute, and now versed in Mediterranean oil and gas policy, Papadopoulos worked as an energy consultant in London.

A few months later, Papadopoulos realized his goal of working for a presidential campaign—he took a job as an advisor with Ben Carson's. But this would be a short-time gig. Carson may have been a likable guy and conservatively solid, but his campaign was dying. It just couldn't capture the zeitgeist like Trump's, so, like the accomplished doctor he is, on March 4, 2016, Carson pulled the plug.

Papadopoulos, unable to get work with Trump's campaign and now out of work after just a couple of months with Carson's, received an out-of-the-blue message on LinkedIn that, unknown to him at the time, set off the chain reaction that would turn his life over under sideways down.

The message was from the London Centre for International Law Practice (LCILP)—an organization claiming to promote "peace and development through international law and dispute resolution." They offered Papadopoulos a job as a director in the company, which he found odd—later telling Fox News he thought it sounded like a front company and a front job. In some ways, it was—the LCILP didn't advertise how well-connected it was to Western intelligence agencies. Nevertheless, Papadopoulos accepted the job offer. "I landed in a coveted position and suddenly found myself in a world filled with influence peddlers who seem to have stepped out of the pages of 'The Maltese Falcon' and 'Jason Bourne' novels," he would write in his book.[4] "Almost everyone I met—and I found this out much later—had ties to intelligence outfits." It's important to note here that he said no Russians worked for the company.

Also of no small measure of importance is that no one outside of LCILP seemed to know exactly what it did. No one knew of any actual law being practiced there, which gave plausibility to Papadopoulos's assertion that it seemed like a front for something else.

Even though he lived in London and worked for LCILP, Papadopoulos never stopped pushing toward working with the Trump campaign. Then in March 2016, after relentlessly emailing Lewandowski, Papadopoulos got his shot—he was hired to work with them as an unpaid adviser on foreign policy. When he went to his bosses at LCILP, Nagi Idris and Peter Dovey, and told them about it, they were livid. They loathed Trump, didn't believe he'd win, and considered it a waste of time. Still, they asked Papadopoulos to attend a conference with them at Link Campus University (LCU) in Rome to meet people they said would help the campaign. Though he wanted to get back to the United States to begin his new assignment with the Trump team, Papadopoulos accepted.

That was the mistake of his life.

Attending the conference triggered events that would ultimately send Papadopoulos to prison. He should have seen it coming. When the Trump-hating bosses of a company with a murky mission like LCILP suddenly about-face and offer to help, one must question everything. Maybe it was unbridled optimism, maybe a consequence of youth, but Papadopoulos trusted his bosses. He couldn't have known what he was walking into was like a line from a Christopher Pike novel, "nothing is as it seems."

Nothing was as it seemed.

LCILP had an agenda, and Link Campus University wasn't exactly about traditional academics. The school was founded in the late '90s by a couple of men fascinated with espionage—the former president of Italy Francesco Cossiga and the former president of Malta Guido de Marco.[5] LCU is home to the Center for Intelligence Research and Safe Society, whose focus is the development of innovative approaches to strategic intelligence. The school often brought in guest lecturers from the CIA and FBI, once offered a master's degree in intelligence, and today has a master's course taught half in Rome and half in Moscow. It's not far-fetched to surmise that, in a lot of ways, LCU was a "spy school."

These were the people Papadopoulos's anti-Trump bosses wanted him to meet because they could be of "help."

At the conference, Idris introduced Papadopoulos to a professor named Joseph Mifsud—a guy who claimed to be a major player with contacts worldwide. He offered to be Papadopoulos's "in" with anyone who was anyone in the diplomatic community. What Mifsud offered would be invaluable to a guy like Papadopoulos. The guy had just taken a job as a foreign policy advisor; how could he *not* want to make some important international contacts?

Mifsud offered to set up a meeting between Putin and Trump. Just like that.

Papadopoulos had just signed on with the Trump campaign. Within a couple of weeks, with no effort whatsoever, he was able to land a meeting for Trump with Russia's president?

For Papadopoulos, that should have raised more than one red flag.

Mifsud's lawyer, Stephan Roh, would later say the idea for Mifsud to introduce Papadopoulos to his supposed Russian contacts came from both Idris and the head of LCU, Vincenzo Scotti, a former Minister of Foreign Affairs of Italy. If that's true, then clearly Papadopoulos was being set up. "I was the right guy to become the wrong man. A guy set up to become the patsy in an international espionage conspiracy," Papadopoulos later reckoned.[6]

Mifsud, due in no small part to special counsel Robert Mueller and a complicit media, has been cast as a shadowy Russian asset who was well-connected to higher-ups in the Russian government—but truth be told, his connections weren't with the Russians, they were with the intelligence community in the West. To think he could set up a meeting with Putin was an absurdist notion at best and clinical delusion at worst. The closest Mifsud came was introducing Papadopoulos to a student named Olga Polonskaya—and depending on who tells the story, Papadopoulos may have been led to believe she was Putin's niece. She's not.

But Papadopoulos kept pushing Mifsud. He wanted a meeting for Trump. So, Mifsud introduced Papadopoulos, through email, to Ivan Timofeev, the Director of Programs at the Russian International Affairs Council (RIAC). It's a think tank calling itself "a link between the state, scholarly community, business, and civil society in an effort to find foreign policy solutions to complex conflict issues." The term "think tank" is essentially a casual way of referring to a policy institute—there isn't a group of people, elbows on the conference table, hands on the forehead, with furrowed brows, grimacing, "Man, I'm trying to think of something, but I got nothing. What about you? You got anything? Think. Think!" Although, perhaps in this case, there was a group united in the thought, "Let's use this greenhorn Papadopoulos to wreck Trump."

Timofeev tells Papadopoulos he's got contacts and offers to meet. They never do.

But Papadopoulos would meet again with Mifsud—April 26, 2016, to be exact. During this meeting, Mifsud dropped the fifty-megaton nuke that would obliterate Papadopoulos's life as he knew it and set off Crossfire Hurricane. He tells him Russia has "dirt" on Hillary Clinton in the form of thousands of her emails.

What a revelation! But maybe Mifsud had been reading *The New York Times* that week. Three days earlier, in an op-ed,[7] Nicholas Kristof floated the idea, "Clinton's private server may have been penetrated by the Russians." Point being, Mifsud's "revelation" wasn't one. Anyone could have claimed—as many pundits did—that Russia had gotten hold of Clinton's email.

Everyone knew about her email. It was in the news cycle even as Papadopoulos and Mifsud had their little chat. We knew that when Clinton was secretary of state, she decided to conduct government business on a private email server installed in her home basement—which was a real problem in terms of protecting information related to national security.

Three years earlier, sensitive emails sent to her by an aide were stolen by a Romanian hacker nicknamed "Guccifer." And even after that hack, and after those emails were published by Russia's RT, Clinton inexplicably still used that email account. The FBI was investigating her possible mishandling of classified information and also whether any foreign enemies of the United States were able to compromise the server. Clinton had deleted more than thirty thousand emails before turning over to the FBI what was left of her State Department email. Now that she was running for president, this raised legitimate concerns about her judgment. For Mifsud to claim he knew Russia had thousands of Clinton's emails was a very big deal—if he was telling the truth.

Papadopoulos maintains he was horrified by the revelation and disgusted by the idea Russia would hack into the email accounts of someone who could be the next president of the United States. He wanted no part of the discussion and didn't ask Mifsud to elaborate. At that point, he thought Mifsud was some sort of plant. According to Papadopoulos, less than a week later, Tobias Ellwood, Britain's Under-Secretary of State for Foreign Affairs, reached out to him. Two days after that, Papadopoulos said he was contacted by two London-based officials from the Defense Intelligence Agency.

Suddenly, a lot of people seemed interested in getting to know Papadopoulos—including an Australian diplomat named Alexander Downer—all after one supposedly private conversation with Mifsud.

Mifsud has since gone back into the shadows—no one has seen or heard from him since the release of the Mueller Report—although his name would later surface in connection with accusations by Flynn's lawyer that two of his cell phones were used in the plot to entrap Flynn.

As for Downer, the Australian High Commissioner to the United Kingdom—one of his advisors, an underling named Erika Thompson, contacted Papadopoulos. Downer wanted to meet him. This was a couple of days after Papadopoulos caused a bit of a ruckus, both in Britain and at Trump campaign headquarters, after London's *The Times* published an interview in which he implied then-Prime Minister David Cameron owed Trump an apology for making negative comments about him.

Downer, Thompson, and Papadopoulos got together at a chichi London wine bar. To hear Papadopoulos describe it,[8] Downer was exactly that—a downer. He was aloof, condescending, curt, and dismissive—and quite possibly recording their entire conversation on his phone. Downer would later claim he asked Papadopoulos about Russia and Trump, and Papadopoulos offered up that the Russians had a "dirt" file on Clinton filled with DNC email. Papadopoulos has said he doesn't recall that exchange—at all. Regardless, Downer reports to Australian intelligence what he alleges Papadopoulos told him.

Neither Downer nor the Australians took Papadopoulos's supposed comments all that seriously—until WikiLeaks unloaded a cache of Clinton's stolen private email onto the web and unleashed an excremental tempest from which Papadopoulos could not escape clean. Australia now decides to loop the United States into Downer's claims, and a week later, the FBI launches Crossfire Hurricane.

Downer's motivation to rat out a Trump advisor by suggesting he was a Russian ally would have been clear to anyone who bothered to look. He was a huge supporter of Hillary Clinton. In 2006, Downer secured a $25 million donation from the Australian government to the Clinton Foundation.[9] The FBI never bothered to share his connection to Clinton with anyone—least of all, Congress.

The FBI painted a surrealist portrait that the stolen Clinton emails were the same ones Downer claimed Papadopoulos told him about—which implied that Papadopoulos had advance knowledge of them. To find out how they were hacked, the DNC hired a cybersecurity technology company called CrowdStrike. It determined the breach came from Russia. So, using the FBI's patented pretzel logic—the same logic it would later apply to Flynn—this meant Papadopoulos, ergo, Trump, was an agent of Russia.

That's quite a stretch, even for the FBI.

Papadopoulos did himself no favors by meeting both before and after the election with the Russia-connected Sergei Millian. The American businessman from Belarus—a source for the bogus Steele Dossier—first contacted Papadopoulos on LinkedIn and, leveraging his position as former head of the Russian American Chamber of Commerce, offered to help the Trump campaign. They met a few times in New York and Chicago. At one meeting, Papadopoulos says Millian offered him $30,000 a month to work as a public relations consultant for an enterprise funded by a former Russian energy minister, but only if he was working for Trump at the same time.[10] He wasn't sure if Millian was wearing a wire but found it odd he was sweating in the Chicago cold. After Trump won the election, Papadopoulos accepted another get-together invite from Millian. This time, Millian's colleague offered up an eye-opening factoid—Millian worked with the FBI.

But Millian wasn't the only one who'd made strange overtures to Papadopoulos. A professor at Cambridge University named Stefan Halper, working as an FBI informant, asked him if the Trump campaign would be open to Russia helping it. According to the 2019 inspector general's report, Papadopoulos rejected that suggestion, telling Halper accepting help from Russia would be "illegal."

On January 27, 2017, Millian was outed as a source for the Steele Dossier by *The Wall Street Journal*.[11] Three days later, FBI investigators finally got around to interviewing

Papadopoulos—six months after the start of Crossfire Hurricane. It didn't take them long to figure out a few things that should have ended the Papadopoulos investigation then and there…

- Papadopoulos had no Russian contacts.
- Without Russian contacts, Papadopoulos couldn't be the one getting the "dirt" on Clinton.
- The FBI informant assigned to both Papadopoulos and Carter Page—a former Cambridge University professor named Stefan Halper—had come up with nothing incriminating.
- In secretly recorded conversations between Papadopoulos and FBI informants, he declared his innocence more than once.
- Papadopoulos's emails, text messages, and internet browser history turned up nothing criminal.

Despite this, the FBI continued and never bothered sharing this evidence with the DOJ.

The reality is this: Papadopoulos was a young, inexperienced political newbie who was in way, way over his head. He'd only met Trump one time. Papadopoulos's only real crime was being so myopically enthusiastic about impressing Trump that he trusted people he shouldn't have.

In the end, after working so feverishly to paint Papadopoulos as a linchpin of foreign intrigue, all the FBI could nail him for was a single, relatively insignificant lie he told investigators—that Mifsud told him about the Russian emails *before* he began working for the Trump campaign, when, in truth, it was after.

It was a basic perjury trap. When investigators asked Papadopoulos the question about when he met Mifsud, they already knew the answer.

Papadopoulos pleaded guilty to lying to the FBI and served twelve days in federal prison. And for what? Papadopoulos didn't really do anything for Trump. His youthful exuberance was merely chum for ravenous Deep State sharks with an insatiable appetite for innocent prey.

CHAPTER 12

PAUL MANAFORT

Paul Manafort is a disbarred lawyer, convicted felon, and former prison inmate—none of which could be said *before* he got involved with the Trump campaign.

Manafort was the campaign's chairman, having won a power struggle with the previous campaign manager, Corey Lewandowski, that ended with Lewandowski's termination. Manafort was hired to lead the campaign's efforts in corralling delegates. As a strategist, and with his long tenure in politics dating back to the Gerald Ford presidency, it was simply a matter of time before he would assume control of the whole thing—and later, without warning, get caught in a web spun by Robert Mueller.

While he's a seasoned political beast now, Manafort's initial foray into politics in the '70s could be described as

"Papadopoulos on steroids"—a brash twenty-something go-getter, with hyped confidence and a mastery of (to use a Trumpism) the "art of the deal." He went out and staked his claim. After graduating from Georgetown Law in 1974, Manafort went to work as an advisor for the Ford campaign while, at the same time, working at a private law firm. The presidential campaigns for which he'd go on to work are quite the who's who of Republicans: Ford, Reagan, Bush 41, Dole, and Trump. Three out of five ain't bad.

Manafort cut against the grain, working for Ford against the advice of his young Republican colleagues who knew Ford was a weak candidate and wouldn't be elected to a full term. Manafort didn't care. Even after Ford lost to Jimmy Carter, he kept a scorecard of who stuck by him and who didn't, licked his wounds, and got back in the game—but this time, on his own terms.

He partnered with his friend, another young, ultraconservative go-getter named Roger Stone, and their friend Charles Black. They started a revolutionary political firm that ignored convention by being both a consulting *and* lobbying firm. It was determined that they could have both political influence and make a ton of money.

They set up shop across the Potomac in Arlington, Virginia, and called the company Black, Manafort & Stone. They'd later rename it Black, Manafort, Stone & Kelly (BMSK) after adding a partner—a Democrat named Peter Kelly, who, at the time, was the DNC's finance chairman. Landing a political power hitter from the other side of the aisle gave BMSK a distinct leg up on other consulting firms—they were bipartisan. A first.

As they'd hoped, BMSK began making money hand over fist. But over the years, many of the people with whom they did business weren't exactly Boy Scouts. The firm earned millions from politicians, corporate clients, foreign governments, and, most troubling, a gallery of rapscallions that came to be known as "The Torturers' Lobby"—tyrannical despots and dictators with horrid records for human rights abuses. BMSK advised Ferdinand Marcos of the Philippines, Mobutu Sese Seko of the Democratic Republic of Congo, and Angolan guerrilla fighter, Jonas Savimbi—a man hailed by Ronald Reagan as a "freedom fighter" but considered a terrorist at home. Savimbi was the principal reason for Angola's virtually nonstop civil war—it lasted twenty-seven years and caused the deaths of nearly one million people. A report by the Institute of Policy Studies called Savimbi "the principal spoiler of the Angolan elections and United Nations-backed peace plans in the early 1990s."[12]

The Philippines deal with Marcos was the first overt sign that Manafort had a special way of doing business where his ends of attaining big money justified his means of getting it. He made that deal—with a Marcos front company—without Kelly's knowledge. Kelly was infuriated when he found out.

At the time, he was working with a Filipino group fighting for democracy, and this wasn't just a conflict of interest—it was wildly humiliating. Kelly had to quit working for them, and BMSK pulled out of that particular contract worth nearly a million dollars. BMSK still had a lucrative relationship with the Philippines, the details of which could fill a book all their own. And to this day, speculation percolates through the swamp that Marcos paid Manafort millions of dollars outside of that deal, possibly $10 million in cash in a couple of suitcases—an assertion he says is "totally fiction."[13]

BMSK may have killed the Marcos deal, but Manafort and his partners were still reaping millions from the "torturers." The Center for Public Integrity says, in 1991 alone, BMSK pulled in more than $3 million from Nigeria, Kenya, the Philippines (Marcos), and Angola's rebel group (Savimbi). All four of them engaged in human rights abuses, and all four of them received monetary aid from the United States. Their combined abuses comprise a laundry list of depravity and cruelty: forced child labor, child prostitution, state-sanctioned rape, torture, human trafficking, and the execution of homosexuals.

But their checks didn't bounce, so as far as Manafort and BMSK were concerned, "Nothing to see here."

BMSK did maintain it recognized concerns for human rights abuses[14] and that it did try to open a dialogue with those countries—although there isn't evidence they did that nor that it made any difference if they did. However, the company isn't solely to blame for doing business with tyrants—during the Reagan and Bush 41 years, the United States often aligned itself with unsavory governments if they mutually stood against communism.

Before Manafort and BMSK made deals with despots, they built the company on financially lucrative deals with all manner of politicians and huge corporations, including an up and coming real estate developer named Donald Trump. Throughout the '80s, money was pouring into BMSK, and as their bank account grew, so did their clout—especially with foreign leaders wanting to boost their profiles with the power brokers of DC, and they paid handsomely.

In 1991, the partners sold BMSK to Burson-Marsteller (now Burson Cohn and Wolfe), which was the second largest public-relations firm in the world. Manafort, Stone, Black, and Kelly all stayed with the company they'd founded—until Manafort left five years later to start his own new company—Davis, Manafort & Friedman.

As he became more successful, Manafort's taste for the high life grew. He collected expensive cars, custom-tailored suits, and luxury real-estate (including a residence in Trump Tower) like mohair sweaters collect lint. As that appetite for excess grew, so did Manafort's thirst for influence. He'd made himself into an international powerbroker, and it didn't seem to matter where the money came from. Manafort wasn't restrained by moral limits—he had none. Besides his roster of politicos, CEOs, and sketchy oligarchs, Manafort's client list now included arms dealers. In the early 2000s, he and Abdul Rahman Al Assir, an arms dealer Manafort first met in the '80s, arranged for a financially strapped biometrics firm to get a cash infusion from a Portuguese bank—the deal destroyed the bank and the biometrics firm failed, but Manafort walked away with more than $1 million by selling the stock in the firm he'd bought before it went belly up.

From that point on—from 2004 until the time he went to work for the Trump campaign—Manafort's wheeling and dealing was a tornadic blur of dubious deals with questionable characters. He was hired by a Russian industrialist and billionaire named Oleg Deripaska—an ally of Putin and well-connected in Russian government circles—and financier Nat Rothschild—more formally known as Nathaniel Philip Victor James Rothschild—to look into the brewing political unrest in the Ukraine, see how it would affect the financial aspects of their business dealings, and help them navigate through it.

A pro-Russian politician named Viktor Yanukovych won the 2004 Ukrainian presidential election, which, to use the most basic term, was a fiasco. The results triggered what became known as the Orange Revolution—Ukrainians took to the streets in protest, claiming the run-off election was rigged through widespread corruption, including voter fraud and intimidation. A Ukrainian court invalidated the results, and a re-vote was ordered. After the votes were counted,

Yanukovych was out and Viktor Yushchenko was in—though Yanukovych would succeed him six years later. Yanukovych then hired Manafort as an advisor and tasked him with fixing his image following the Orange Revolution. Yanukovych would play a big role in Manafort's later troubles.

Meantime, Manafort doubled back to Deripaska—with whom he reportedly[15] had a $10 million annual contract—and worked on a plan to "greatly benefit the Putin government" by "influencing politics, business dealings, and media in the United States and Europe." Manafort denied his work with Deripaska was ever pro-Russian in nature.[16] Deripaska later sued Manafort to recover the roughly $19 million Deripaska gave him for the purchase of a telecommunications company in Ukraine that never went through, and for not explaining to Deripaska how the money was spent.

Manafort continued to consult for Yanukovych and not only helped his pro-Russian party gain a number seats in the Ukrainian parliament, but also helped Yanukovych win the presidency in 2010. But that's when Yanukovych apparently stopped listening to him.

Yanukovych lost the presidency four years later after he pulled Ukraine from a deal he'd made with the European Union that would have distanced Ukraine from Russia and bettered its relationship with the West. The capital city of Kyiv exploded with riots and violence, and the streets filled with outrage resembling a modern-day ANTIFA demonstration in the streets of Portland—except the authorities in Kyiv did something about it—and it was lethal. Ukrainian security forces opened fire, killing dozens of people.

Why would Yanukovych order the use of such deadly force? Some speculate Manafort advised him to. The loudest voice in that bunch is a Ukrainian lawyer representing the victims of those shootings. But let's be real. Manafort has been called many things, but "murderer" has never been among them. Although the optics weren't helped when a hacker accessed text messages between Manafort's daughters and one of them suggested, "You know he has killed people in Ukraine? Knowingly. As a tactic to outrage the world and get focus on Ukraine. Remember when there were all those deaths taking place. A while back. About a year ago. Revolts and what not. Do you know whose strategy that was to cause that, to send those people out and get them slaughtered?"[17] Manafort probably still has the tire tracks on his back after being thrown under that bus.

To be clear, there is absolutely no evidence of any kind to suggest Manafort ever did, or ever would, recommend the massacre of civilians.

The real question was how in the world did this guy from New Britain, Connecticut, a self-made man who'd established himself as a big-time player in Washington's power circles, find himself attached to a murderous, corrupt Cold War–era villain cast straight from the pages of an Ian Fleming novel?

Was it all just for the money? There was a lot of it. Yanukovych paid Manafort millions—which the FBI would note in 2016 when they began investigating him for tax fraud and money laundering.

As for Yanukovych, he snuck out of Ukraine and became a fugitive when prosecutors criminally charged him for mass murder of the demonstrators. He took refuge in Russia, where he remains to this day.

The work Manafort did for Yanukovych and the Ukraine's Party of Regions raised flags for the FBI well before Manafort joined the Trump campaign. Agents interviewed him in March 2013 and in July 2014, when they also interviewed his second in command, Rick Gates. They also put him under electronic surveillance, which continued even after the 2016 election.[18] But when Manafort signed on with Trump, that's when he joined Papadopoulos, Page, and Flynn on the list of targets for the Trump-loathing FBI agent Peter Strzok. After all, Manafort did business with Ukrainians and people connected with Russia, so for someone like Strzok, who was virulently anti-Trump and really into pushing the whole "Russian collusion" thing, this was like tossing a ribeye to a salivating Rottweiler.

But for Manafort, from that point on in mid-2014 through to his joining the Trump campaign in 2016, the pressures took a toll from which he'd barely recover—Manafort was now borrowing against the equity in several of his real-estate holdings, and Deripaska's lawyers, seven years after first filing a lawsuit against him, were back in court demanding he provide more information about that uncompleted Ukrainian deal. Manafort suffered an emotional breakdown and checked himself into a psychiatric care facility in Arizona.

Like they say, "You ride her until she bucks you."

But like they also say, "You've got to get back on the horse." And he did.

After his treatment, Manafort left the Arizona facility and returned to DC. He joined the Trump campaign in March 2016, but nary a month went by and a DNC consultant was already digging for dirt on him, in particular his dealings in the Ukraine. She reportedly met with officials at the Ukrainian Embassy in Washington. In July, Strzok launched Crossfire Hurricane—remember, the operation he wrote and authorized himself—initially targeting Manafort, Page, and Papadopoulos. Flynn would come later.

Then the bottom fell out for Manafort—again.

The New York Times broke a story alleging that a ledger found in Kyiv showed Manafort received undisclosed cash payments of $12.7 million from Ukraine's pro-Russia Party of Regions while he was working for Yanukovych.[19] Manafort was incensed by the report and issued a statement obtained by NBC News lambasting the paper. He denied having received any cash payments and accused the paper of ignoring facts to fit its political agenda. "I have never received a single 'off-the-books cash payment' as falsely reported by *The New York Times*, nor have I ever done work for the governments of Ukraine or Russia," Manafort said.[20] "The suggestion that I accepted cash payments is unfounded, silly and nonsensical." He pointed out that there was no evidence of any cash payments and that every Ukrainian government official interviewed in the piece said Manafort hadn't done anything wrong. He also took a moment to get in a dig at Hillary Clinton. "The *Times* does fail to disclose the fact that the Clinton Foundation has taken (and may still take) payments in exchange for favors from Hillary Clinton while serving as Secretary of State."

Touché.

Clinton did sell one-fifth of America's uranium rights to Russia for a roughly $145 million "donation" to the Clinton Foundation in a nifty scheme likely to impress any seasoned grifter. Here's how it worked—a Russian atomic energy company bought a Canadian company called Uranium One, which gave Moscow 20 percent of all uranium production capacity in the United States. Clinton, as secretary of state, had to approve the deal, which she did. Then, as if by magic, money started pouring into the bank accounts of the Clinton Foundation donated by a foundation run by the family of Uranium One's CEO. For good measure and (cough) by coincidence, husband Bill was paid a half-million dollars for a speech in Moscow by a bank promoting stock in Uranium One.

So, again, touché.

As for Manafort, something had to give, and five days after *The New York Times* published its story, he resigned from the Trump campaign.

His resignation wasn't necessarily due to that report, though. Manafort was more likely forced out after a staff shake-up that saw Kellyanne Conway promoted to campaign manager and Steven Bannon, formerly of Breitbart, brought in as campaign CEO.

A little more than a year later, Mueller would rear his ugly head and charge both Manafort and his right-hand man, Richard Gates, with tax fraud, conspiracy, money laundering, failing to report foreign bank accounts to the federal government, lying to the federal government, and a crime that is almost never prosecuted: failure to register as foreign agents.

Of note: The crimes for which Manafort was accused were committed long before he'd ever been involved in the Trump campaign, so whatever he may have done had absolutely nothing to do with Trump. The indictment itself proved Manafort's alleged crimes predated his work on the campaign and showed no collusion whatsoever between Trump and Russia—nor any collusion between Manafort and Russia either.

Manafort would be convicted on eight of eighteen counts for this set of charges. In a second case, he pleaded guilty as part of a plea bargain for failing to register as a foreign agent while conducting lobbying work for the Ukraine and for witness tampering. Manafort admitted to making false statements on loan applications and failing to report $15 million in income for his work in Ukraine. He also copped to using foreign banks and shell companies to hide that income.

Not a single one of these crimes involved Trump.

Not a single one of these crimes showed collusion with Russia.

Between his two cases, Manafort was sentenced to a little more than seven years in prison, though he was released after about a year because of the Coronavirus pandemic. He'll serve the rest of his sentence at home.

All of this could have been avoided.

But Crossfire Hurricane.

Manafort's lawyer, Kevin Downing, told *The Washington Times* he and Manafort met with the FBI, turned over Manafort's tax documents, and were working toward resolving any tax issues with a noncriminal settlement, but then the Russia probe came along.[21]

Manafort's fate was sealed the minute the first corrupt FBI agent added his name to the list of targets and falsely smeared him as an agent of Russia.

Strzok, Comey, Mueller, and the rest of the dirty cops may have taken down Manafort, Page, and Papadopoulos, but they had yet to bag the biggest prey of them all.

However, they had a plan and a trap, and some help from the Oval Office.

ACT 4

CROSSFIRE RAZOR, A.K.A. “THE FRAME JOB”

CHAPTER 13

THE OVAL OFFICE MEETING

As the new year dawned in January of 2017, both panic and malaise settled into the offices at 1600 Pennsylvania Avenue. In less than three weeks, Donald Trump would be sworn in and moved in, and despondency wafted through the halls like the angel of death passing through Egypt.

This big-talking billionaire with a penchant for PR had already vowed to a populist base that establishment politics were over and that soon he'd unravel eight years of what Obama had worked so hard to accomplish—the Iran nuclear deal, the Paris climate accord, "concessions" to Cuba, racial and economic division, business-stifling regulatory practices, and the biggest white elephant of them all, Obamacare.

A few months earlier, no one in the Obama camp gave much thought to how they'd handle a Trump presidency—they didn't think he'd win. Hillary Clinton was the anointed successor, and Obama's legacy was ensured. But as the neophyte politician began transitioning in, malaise gave way to a panicked awakening.

"We need to stop this guy."

They also needed to stop Obama's old nemesis from the DIA, the incoming national security advisor. In his new role, Flynn would uncover Crossfire Hurricane and how the Obama administration used a dossier filled with bogus information secretly paid for by Hillary Clinton to falsely accuse Trump of treasonous actions with Russia and to ruin his campaign, and later, his presidency. Plus, Flynn would likely catch on to every other shady deal orchestrated by the administration. With the clock ticking in the waning days of their reign, Obama and his loyalists set about nailing Flynn before he could nail them.

On January 5 came the meeting where Obama took charge of taking down Flynn. On that day, the Oval Office was a popular place. Anybody who was anybody was there. We know, from declassified court papers (from the Flynn filings in appeals court, which we'll discuss later) there was a high-level meeting—a "who's who" of the administration—which included Obama; Vice President Joe Biden; FBI Director James Comey; the crooked Deputy Assistant Director of the FBI's counterintelligence division, Peter Strzok; Deputy Attorney General, Sally Yates; a couple of cloak and dagger guys (CIA Director John Brennan and the Director of National Intelligence James Clapper); National Security Advisor Susan Rice (whom Flynn would be replacing); and some others from the National Security Council.

Comey, Brennan, Yates, and Clapper were there to brief the administration on the assessment into whether Russia interfered in the 2016 U.S. elections. There was nothing nefarious about that. But following the meeting, as the assembled began to filter out, Obama asked Comey and Yates to stay behind with him, Biden, and Rice. What followed was a meeting in which the most powerful man in the world directed a political hit on Flynn.

This was La Cosa Nostra—the family planning to whack a rival, with Obama as the don, Comey the consigliere, and Strzok the capo.

Explosive handwritten notes by none other than Strzok reveal both Obama and Biden not only knew about the investigation into Flynn but advised how to do it. The notes came to light in a federal court filing by the DOJ in 2020. We now have the "smoking gun" proving the case against Flynn was a trap, and Obama and Biden were in on it.

To paraphrase Kevin Bacon's "Captain Ross" character in *A Few Good Men*, it's obvious their intention was to smear a high-ranking Trump staffer in the desperate hope that the mere appearance of impropriety would wreck Flynn and protect them.

The irony? The FBI had already tried and failed to label Flynn a Russian agent. Strzok had opened an investigation six months earlier in August 2016, dubbing it "Crossfire Razor"—the code name they'd assigned to Flynn. In the electronic communication Strzok submitted to launch the investigation, he detailed why Flynn was an FBI target: "Crossfire Razor may wittingly or unwittingly be involved in activity on behalf of the Russian Federation which may constitute a federal crime or threat to national security."

A thirty-three-year military veteran with an unblemished record of service who was once the most powerful military intelligence officer in the world—a man who'd spent nearly all of his adult life fighting the spread of communism and terrorism was now a "threat to national security?" Just what pray tell were the reasons for that? According to Strzok's paperwork, there were three: Flynn had signed on as a foreign policy advisor to the Trump campaign, he had connections to "state-affiliated entities," and he'd traveled to Russia in 2015. Not listed was *why* Flynn travelled to Russia—to attend the RT television network gala.

Flynn's connection to "state-run entities" was his speaking engagement at RT and the Flynn Intelligence Group's work for a Russian air cargo company and an American-based security company that was a subsidiary of a Russian cybersecurity firm.

So, on the basis of working for Trump, attending one gala in Moscow, and work done by his now-defunct business, Flynn was "involved in activity on behalf of the Russian Federation." This wasn't just, "He's *connected* to Russia." No, the accusation was Flynn worked "*on behalf*" of Russia, which would make him an agent of Russia. For the entire second half of 2016, Flynn was an unsuspecting target of an FBI investigation.

This isn't to be confused with the unrelated 2016 DOJ investigation into the Flynn Intel Group's work with a Turkish businessman who allegedly had ties to an energy executive with connections to the Kremlin. Remember when they tried unsuccessfully to prove Flynn's partner in FIG was an agent of Turkey?

The FBI knew Flynn wasn't a Russian agent. Strzok knew it. He didn't care. In fact, the day before that Oval Office meeting, he stopped the FBI from closing the Flynn investigation after its field office in DC sent out a communication saying it was terminating Crossfire Razor. The bureau determined there was no derogatory information on Flynn and that he was "no longer a viable candidate as part of the larger Crossfire Hurricane umbrella case."

That should have been the end of it.

However, Strzok was so resolute with his anti-Trump agenda, the very same day the FBI told its agents it was ending the investigation, he told the case manager to keep it open, texting, "Hey, don't close Razor." Strzok implied the FBI brass (likely Comey) was involved in the decision and still needed to decide what to do with him. He also used the recordings of Flynn's conversations with Kislyak as the premise to keep the investigation open.

Yes, the FBI secretly recorded three of Flynn's phone conversations he'd had with the Russian ambassador in late December. The FBI will tell you it was part of their routine protocol to electronically monitor any calls between Russian and American officials. They found nothing whatsoever incriminating in those recordings. Strzok's notes regarding the Oval Office meeting on January 5 reveal Comey told the room Flynn's calls "appear legit."

Of course they were legitimate. Flynn was working through Kislyak to mitigate the tensions caused by the Obama sanctions. We don't know why the FBI reversed course on closing Crossfire Razor, but we do know both Obama and Biden both took part in keeping it open.

After the core meeting in the Oval Office, Obama, Biden, Comey, Yates, and Rice gathered for the second meeting. A couple of weeks later, Rice documented it in a memo she emailed to herself on, of all days, Trump's inauguration day. She recalled Obama began the meeting by saying he'd "learned of the information about Flynn" regarding the wiretapped calls and Flynn's conversation with Kislyak about the Russian sanctions. He wondered aloud whether they should be treating Flynn differently given the information they now had vis-à-vis if he was working with Russia. Maybe some matters shouldn't be shared with him during the transition. Yates heard this and was caught completely off guard—this was the first time she'd heard anything about those recorded calls. How is it the deputy attorney general of the United States didn't know the FBI was secretly recording the incoming national security advisor's calls, unless the FBI had gone rogue with its own agenda?

It is clear that Obama already knew about the wiretapped calls.

Rice's email to herself read more like a "cover your ass" kind of note than it did a fully formed reckoning of the meeting. While putting the onus on Obama for leading things, she did make a point to note he wanted to keep the investigation "by the book," a phrase she also attributed to Comey. Writing and sending a lengthy email to yourself on the same day the new president is sworn into office in which you mostly talk about how "by the book" your boss is? That is in no way fishy.

Strzok's notes from that second Oval Office were damning to Obama and Biden—although it is curious how he could write notes about it since no one other than the people present knows whether Strzok was actually there. There's no record of it. Perhaps he *was* there, or the more likely scenario is he'd received a briefing on it. Regardless, those incriminating notes, which Strzok likely never thought the public would see, show that Obama, Biden, Comey, Yates, and Rice talked about the content of Flynn's calls with Kislyak and how to move forward with the case against him. Obama made it clear he wanted the "right people" working the investigation. Biden suggested using the Logan Act.

It's just so perfectly Joe Biden to pull the Logan Act from the mothballs—it's a law dating back to the John Adams presidency. Passed in 1799, the Logan Act is almost never, ever used—and it might not even be constitutional. The law makes it illegal for a private citizen to discuss United States foreign policy with a foreign government. The sole reason for its existence? In 1798, a former Pennsylvania state legislator named George Logan tried on his own to negotiate a peace settlement between the U.S. and France to end the Quasi-War. To be clear, while the Logan Act does prevent *private* citizens from engaging in foreign policy talks with foreign governments, it does *not* prevent an incoming national security advisor from doing so. Yet that's what Biden, Obama, Comey, and the rest of the conspirators hung their hats on to get rid of Flynn.

In 221 years, there have been just two prosecutions under the Logan Act, and both were in the 1800s.

It's a real jurisprudential stretch to pull a stale statute from a musty bag of tricks and try to build a case around it. But that's exactly what Biden did.

Three years later, on ABC's *Good Morning America*, he lied about his involvement in the Flynn investigation, telling host George Stephanopoulos, "I was aware that there was—that they had asked for an investigation, but that's all I know about it and I don't think anything else."[1] A month later, the revelation of Strzok's notes busted Biden dead to rights.

What we know from the FBI's notes and the Rice email is that Obama was well aware of Flynn's wiretapped calls with Kislyak, he directed any information about the Flynn case be kept from Trump, and he gave nodding approval to the FBI's moving forward against Flynn.

So now, with their commander-in-chief's blessing and guidance, federal agents went to work on the detailed, spurious trap they'd use to catch their unsuspecting target.

CHAPTER 14

THE AMBUSH

January 6, 2017, the day after that Oval Office meeting, was a typical winter day for New York City—the temperature didn't rise above freezing all day. But the cold and the overnight snow weren't much of a thought for the contingent of government intelligence bigwigs headed toward Trump Tower—they had other things on their minds.

In exactly two weeks, Trump would officially become president. James Comey, CIA Director John Brennan, Director of National Intelligence James Clapper, and NSA head Mike Rogers made their way to 725 5th Avenue to brief Trump on the Intelligence Community Assessment of Russia's efforts to interfere in the 2016 election.

But that wasn't all. They also had another, less noble plan on their agenda.

Once the intelligence briefing with the main players was over, Comey met privately with Trump to reveal the Steele Dossier and one of its extraordinarily salacious allegations—that Russians possessed tapes of Trump having sex with prostitutes in the Presidential Suite of the Ritz-Carlton Moscow four years earlier.

If one didn't know better, you'd think J. Edgar Hoover was running the FBI and not James Comey.

Comey documented the meeting in a summary memo to his deputy Andrew McCabe; McCabe's chief of staff, James Rybicki; and the FBI's general counsel, James Baker. He wrote that Trump denied he'd ever had sex with prostitutes and said he always assumes the hotel rooms in which he stays are "wired" in some way. Comey said he did too.

The private conversation with Trump was meticulously planned. An investigation by the DOJ's inspector general in 2019 revealed there was a group planning meeting that included Comey, McCabe, Rybicki, senior members of the collusion investigation, and Baker. The group decided Comey needed to do the talking and that he had to do it alone to soft-pedal the delivery to lessen the possible embarrassment.

In his notes about the meeting, Comey makes himself sound altruistic, but the FBI's real motivations still haven't been adequately explained. In 2019, the ranking member of the House Intelligence Committee, Representative Devin Nunes of California, told Fox News, "The evidence we have is that Comey wasn't going to brief the president just to get him up to speed. He was acting as if he was an agent working for the Crossfire Hurricane team, so that is clear evidence that he was involved in this, whereas before, he tried to pretend that he's like a step or two away from what happened."[2]

Comey told Trump the sex allegation "might be totally made up," but since it came from Russia, it was the FBI's duty to protect him from "efforts to coerce him." There was one other big, relevant fact Trump would have undoubtedly wanted to know as well—that the dossier was chock-full of unreliable information compiled by a former British spy desperate to keep Trump from becoming president, and that Hillary Clinton and the DNC paid for it.

Comey also couldn't tell him what the inspector general would later find out—that the Crossfire Hurricane team didn't care to learn who paid for the information in the dossier, because they believed if what was in it was true, then it wouldn't matter who paid for it.

Evidently, the FBI had its own special "don't ask, don't tell" policy.

Trump was told the news media—in particular, CNN—had now become aware of the dossier. As Comey noted, Trump couldn't believe they hadn't run with the story.

That would soon change.

What Trump didn't know was that Clapper talked to CNN's Jake Tapper about the dossier and that an associate of the late Senator John McCain, a former assistant secretary of state named David Kramer, leaked the dossier to a dozen media outlets.[3]

Four days after the Trump Tower briefing, CNN reported on pieces of the dossier and that Russia had compromising personal information on Trump. They wouldn't publish all of the dossier, though, because they couldn't independently corroborate the allegations. But BuzzFeed had no such journalistic qualms. They published the dossier in its entirety.

Now an unverified, salacious, and mostly untrue packet of opposition research was running rampant through the news cycle, painting the soon-to-be president as an agent of Russia. Within two days, thanks to another leak, the soon-to-be national security advisor would be caught in that cyclone too.

Someone leaked the Flynn-Kislyak phone call to *The Washington Post*, where it was included in an op-ed piece on January 12. Foreign affairs columnist David Ignatius asked several legitimate questions: "What did Flynn say, and did it undercut the U.S. sanctions? The Logan Act (though never enforced) bars U.S. citizens from correspondence intending to influence a foreign government about 'disputes' with the United States. Was its spirit violated?"[4] Ignatius was right to ask these questions given that he didn't know the dossier was rooted in falsehood, nor did he know of the private Oval Office meeting where Comey said Flynn's calls with Kislyak "appear legit."

The dossier had its intended effect—it sullied the presidency and gave raw meat to a ravenous, biased media complex. MSNBC was obsessed with it. To listen to them (though based on their basement-scraping ratings, not many people do), you'd think Trump was Julius Rosenberg. Every two-bit political prognosticator with a blue-checked Twitter account and a blog was now an intelligence expert weighing in on every media platform that would have them.

For the fanatical anti-Trump faction, Trump wasn't just a Nazi: he was a Russki, too.

A few days after that *Washington Post* op-ed, Vice President Pence appeared on CBS's *Face the Nation*, where he told host John Dickerson that Flynn never discussed the U.S. sanctions on Russia with Kislyak. "General Flynn has been in touch with diplomatic leaders, security leaders in some 30 countries. That's exactly what the incoming national security advisor should do," Pence said, defending Flynn's right to make the calls as part of his job. "What I can confirm, having spoken to him about it, is that those conversations that happened to occur around the time that the United States took action to expel diplomats had nothing whatsoever to do with those sanctions."

Five days after that, Trump took the oath of office as president.

A whirlwind had already swallowed Trump and his team like a Kansas twister gobbling up Dorothy and Toto, and they'd not even officially started their jobs yet.

Trump was just two days into his term, settling into finalizing the members of his team, and Flynn was being sworn in as national security advisor, when *The Wall Street Journal* reported that U.S. counterintelligence agents had been investigating Flynn's communications with Kislyak. This was news to the White House. They didn't know anything about it. Spokeswoman Sarah Sanders issued a statement saying, "We have absolutely no knowledge of any investigation or even a basis for such an investigation."[5]

The other thing they didn't know—the FBI was already in meetings coordinating the perjury trap they would set for Flynn two days later at his office in the White House.

Deputy Director McCabe would send two agents to ambush Flynn—Strzok and Supervisory Special Agent Joe Pientka. They planned meticulously, right down to the exact wording of their conversation and questions. Strzok even put together a list of possible questions Flynn might ask so he could prepare for what his answers would be. He ran the questions by his mistress, FBI attorney Lisa Page, and FBI's general counsel, James Baker. The list of questions included:

- Am I in trouble?
- Am I the subject of an investigation?

- Is it a criminal investigation?
- Is it an espionage investigation?
- Will you tell the White house what I tell you?
- Do I need an attorney?

Strzok asked the lawyers what he should do in the event Flynn asked those questions, or any of the other half dozen on the list. Should he shut Flynn down, hear him out, keep the interview going, or bring another agent into the room?

The FBI's highest level was orchestrating the strategy that would be most effective in setting up Flynn during that meeting. But the team didn't all see eye to eye on what that was. The foot soldiers wanted the interview to come off like a friendly conversation between colleagues, to keep it so conversational that Flynn wouldn't get wise to the fact that he was the target of a criminal investigation. But Bill Priestap, the FBI's chief of counterintelligence, disagreed with that tactic. He argued for the team to reassess its approach and to clearly determine the FBI's objective. In his handwritten notes documenting the meeting with Comey and McCabe, he asked, "What's our goal? Truth, admission or to get him to lie so we can prosecute him or get him fired?"

The FBI was deliberately creating a crime to blame on Flynn. It truly had become the Soviet secret police embodying Lavrentiy Beria's mantra, "Show me the man and I'll show you the crime."

It was disturbingly naked in its villainy.

Priestap did have a secondary angle to get Flynn should the first not work. "If we get him to admit to breaking the Logan Act, give facts to DOJ and have them decide."

This was such an egregious tactic that when the notes came to light in court filings two years later, it stunned many in the legal community. Constitutional law professor Jonathan Turley summed it up best with this Twitter post, "…the reference to the Logan Act is particularly chilling. It suggests the use of a flagrantly unconstitutional act to trap a top Trump official."

Bingo.

On January 24, McCabe called Flynn and asked if agents could come over to his office to chat about the Kislyak calls. Flynn had no problem with that and told McCabe since the FBI monitors those kinds of calls, they probably already knew everything that was said. According to his notes, McCabe told Flynn he wanted to do the interview "quickly, quietly, and as discreetly as possible." So he advised against Flynn having a White House lawyer present because the DOJ would then have to be involved. You don't need to be a regular viewer of *Dateline* to know that when a cop says you don't need a lawyer during questioning, it's a certain sign you're being set up.

Strzok and Pientka made their way over to Flynn's office in the West Wing. He agreed to speak without a lawyer present. Of course he did. Why would Flynn ask for a lawyer when agents he had no reason to distrust (that he knew about) told him he didn't need one?

As they'd planned it, Strzok and Pientka kept the interview light and conversational. Strzok later said Flynn saw the agents as allies, so he was relaxed and unguarded. Neither McCabe nor Strzok and Pientka told Flynn he was under investigation. When asked about the calls with Kislyak, Flynn said he never asked Russia not to retaliate for the sanctions implemented by Obama.

Here's the question that has to be asked. If the FBI already had recordings and full transcripts of the calls between Flynn and Kislyak, then why would they need to ask Flynn what he said? They already knew what he said. As with their interview of Papadopoulos, agents were asking questions for which they already knew the answers. This was another perjury trap. Clearly, if all else failed, the FBI figured they'd get Flynn on a false statements charge.

After the interview, Strzok reported he had the impression Flynn wasn't lying. Notes written by then-Deputy Assistant Attorney General Tashina Gauhar attached to a court filing by Flynn's attorney three years later said Strzok and Pientka believed Flynn was being forthright and truthful during the interview and that he simply didn't remember everything about the calls with Kislyak. And handwritten notes from former FBI general counsel Dana Boente said Flynn couldn't reasonably be prosecuted under the Logan Act, and also that he shouldn't be viewed as "a source of collusion." Meaning the FBI determined Flynn was not a Russian agent and had not violated any laws with the Kislyak calls.

Upon revelation of the bombshell notes in the court filings, Trump was ecstatic. He took to Twitter heralding the news while also digging at the FBI: "New documents just released reveal General Flynn was telling the truth, and the FBI knew it!"

The FBI didn't engage in a single legally just action in the Flynn investigation. His behavior was so void of illegalities the FBI planned to end the investigation on January 4. But when a police force employs corrupt actors dedicated to serving their own biases rather than their community, what's left is the sort of lawlessness they'd sworn to fight.

In August 2020, Former Deputy Attorney General Sally Yates appeared before the Senate Judiciary Committee and blamed Comey for the fiasco. She testified the FBI conducted the Flynn interview without her authorization—and without the knowledge of White House counsel.

She asserted Comey circumvented normal processes by acting unilaterally, and she told Senator Lindsey Graham, when asked, that Comey had gone "rogue."

Yates also admitted that the decision to pursue Flynn was made because the Obama administration had concerns the Trump administration would reverse Obama's newfound policy of confronting Russia. Translation: Obama destroyed an innocent man's reputation and his finances, subjected him to public ridicule and scorn, forced him to sell his home due to crushing legal bills, and left him to face prison time because of a difference of opinion on a foreign policy issue. Few words adequately convey the depth of evil it takes to do something like that.

At the end of all of this, the DOJ would later conclude the FBI's interview of Flynn was unjustified and "conducted without any legitimate investigative basis."

But as it stood in January 2017, for Flynn, the worst was yet to come.

CHAPTER 15

THE TAKEDOWN

Agents Strzok and Pientka left Flynn's office with a problem—they didn't think Flynn was lying. The bureau had expended so much time and energy carefully crafting a plot to catch a guy in a lie that it now had an unexpected conundrum—what do you do when the guy you tried to snare in a perjury trap tells the truth?

For one, if you're the FBI, you don't let it stop you. You find other ways to make it work and allow for some help from other like-minded conspirators.

While Flynn was blissfully unaware of what was happening at the FBI or DOJ regarding his "casual" chat with Strzok and Pientka, Sally Yates, who was now the acting attorney general, along with Mary McCord—the acting assistant attorney general for national security at the DOJ—met with

Trump's White House counsel, Don McGahn, two days after the interview. They told him Flynn was lying about the content of his conversation with Kislyak and that he *did* ask Russia not to escalate its response to the Obama sanctions. They warned McGahn that Flynn was now vulnerable to blackmail by Russia. In a 2020 op-ed she wrote for *The New York Times*, McCord expressed her belief it was important the Trump administration know this.

McCord claimed the DOJ and FBI had differing opinions on the Flynn issue. The FBI preferred to keep what it knew about Flynn close to the chest as it kept investigating, not just as a counterintelligence investigation but also as a criminal one.[6] She and others at the DOJ didn't believe a Logan Act violation could be successfully prosecuted, but they did agree there was a counterintelligence threat to which Trump should be alerted. McCord also essentially confirmed what Yates has since said, that Comey went "rogue" and acted unilaterally when he sent agents to question Flynn without coordinating with the DOJ or following the established protocols for engaging White House officials.

On that same day, according to then-White House press secretary Sean Spicer, McGahn did brief Trump and senior aides about the Flynn situation.

The next day, Yates returned to meet with McGahn, this time without McCord. McGahn asked for the evidence the

FBI had on Flynn. Later, Spicer told reporters McGahn's office reviewed the legal issues and determined "there was not a legal issue but rather a trust issue."

Trump had been in office for a week, and the pan-bangers crying "collusion!" were getting louder. Of course, they had help from a petulant mainstream media composed of left-wing propagandists still sore over Hillary Clinton's election defeat and fueled by animus toward Trump. The seal on the powder keg gave way on February 9 when both *The New York Times* and *The Washington Post* published articles reporting on Flynn's calls with Kislyak and that he'd discussed sanctions with him before Trump took office.

Clearly, someone was leaking classified information to the media, which in and of itself is a serious federal crime.

The *Times* brought up the Logan Act and described the law as "murky," especially if it's applied to people involved in presidential transitions. The paper also reported, "The officials who had read the transcripts acknowledged that while the conversation warranted investigation, it was unlikely, by itself, to lead to charges against a sitting national security adviser."[7]

While the public wouldn't see the transcripts of the Flynn-Kislyak calls until they were declassified and released in May 2020, the FBI and DOJ knew what was in them was fairly innocuous. Yes, Flynn did talk about sanctions, but not as some sort of diplomatic negotiation, nor did Flynn make any promises. The sanctions, by the way, were imposed by Obama because of Russia's alleged interference in the 2016 presidential elections. It was clear Flynn made a simple request that Kislyak talk to the Kremlin to temper Russia's reaction to the sanctions. Flynn recognized Obama was likely to expel Russians from the United States and wanted to quell any issue before it began. "They're gonna dismiss some number of Russians out of the country, I understand all that…. But what I would ask Russia to do is to not—is—is—if anything—because I know you have to have some sort of action—to, to only make it reciprocal. Make it reciprocal. Don't—don't make it—don't go any further than you have to. Because I don't want us to get into something that has to escalate, on a, you know, on a tit for tat. You follow me, Ambassador?"

Does that seriously seem like a man in quid-pro-quo collusion with a foreign government?

Flynn told Kislyak they could revisit the issue once Trump was in office. "And then what we can do is, when we come in, we can then have a better conversation about where, where we're gonna go, uh, regarding uh, regarding our relationship."

During the follow-up call a couple of days later, Kislyak reported to Flynn that Moscow had agreed to act with "cold heads" (clearly a translation issue) and hoped they could sort things out once Trump took office. "We are hoping within two weeks we will be able to start working in more constructive way," Kislyak told him.

Flynn made no promises. There was no quid-pro-quo.

He also wasn't in violation of the decrepit Logan Act. It was obvious to any sensible person Flynn had not said or done anything remotely improper. He was doing his job.

The FBI and DOJ knew this. That's why they refrained from charging him for violating the Logan Act. But the public didn't have transcripts of the calls; they had to rely on what the media was telling them—that Flynn was a traitor working on behalf of Russia.

The other angle the media played up was the "lie."

Much has been made about whether Flynn did or didn't talk about those sanctions with Kislyak, and whether he lied when asked about it. To borrow a quote from Hillary Clinton—what difference, at this point, does it make?

The FBI had the transcripts. They knew Flynn had spoken about the sanctions during the call. Why even ask whether he did or didn't? Unless, of course, there was an ulterior motive, which we know there was from Bill Priestap's question back at the planning meeting for the Flynn interview: "What's our goal? Truth, admission or to get him to lie so we can prosecute him or get him fired?"

It seems such a ticky-tacky issue of wordplay. *The Washington Post* reported on February 9 that Flynn twice told them he didn't discuss sanctions during the call, but the next day Flynn's spokesperson backed away from the denial. "While he had no recollection of discussing sanctions, he couldn't be certain that the topic never came up."[8]

What difference, at this point, does it make?

The day after the *Post* story was published, Trump told reporters aboard Air Force One he wasn't aware of the reports Flynn had discussed sanctions with Kislyak and that he'd look into it. Interestingly, CNN's story about Trump's comments indicated Flynn's innocence: "The context of Flynn's side of the conversation wasn't clear, even to the FBI and intelligence agencies that reviewed the content, and there's nothing to indicate that Flynn made any promises or acted improperly in the discussion."[9]

"There's nothing to indicate that Flynn made any promises or acted improperly in the discussion."

How much more clear can it be Flynn was being railroaded if even the liberally biased CNN says Flynn hadn't acted improperly?

It didn't matter. On the morning of February 13, Kellyanne Conway told MSNBC that Trump had full confidence in Flynn, but by nightfall, it was over.

Flynn resigned.

In his resignation letter, Flynn said he'd had several calls with foreign counterparts, ministers, and ambassadors to help facilitate a smooth transition and to build necessary relationships between Trump, his advisors, and foreign leaders.

"Unfortunately, because of the fast pace of events, I inadvertently briefed the Vice President-Elect and others with incomplete information regarding my phone calls with the Russian Ambassador," Flynn wrote. "I have sincerely apologized to the President and the Vice President, and they have accepted my apology."

Flynn had nothing to apologize for. Though he may have accepted defeat by resigning, if there's one thing a soldier knows, it's you can lose a battle and still win the war.

And for this general, the war was far from over.

CHAPTER 16

THE CURIOUS CASE OF THE 302

THE AGE IN WHICH WE LIVE IS EASILY THE MOST TECHNOlogically documented in the whole of human history. From a vacation, a party, or a selfie by a narcissist in dire need of validation to riots, lootings, and "peaceful" protests, there's nary an event that escapes the omnipresent lens of a smartphone. Devices like the Amazon Echo, which according to some estimates resides in 60 million homes, have the capability of documenting literally every word spoken in the home, and many people believe they do.

But at the Federal Bureau of Investigation, an agency with near limitless resources and access to every conceivable technological advancement known to man, the preferred method of documenting interviews? Handwritten notes and memory. That's what Strzok and Pientka would rely on to document the interview with Flynn, but as we'll soon learn, Strzok had other ideas.

The FBI protocol for documenting interviews typically goes like this—the investigators and (or) an attorney asks the questions, and an agent takes notes by hand. That agent types up the notes onto Form FD-302, more commonly known as a "302," and has five working days from when the interview was conducted to submit it. The entire reason and sole purpose of the 302 is to document what the agent heard or observed from the suspect or witness. For the record, Flynn didn't know he was either. This has been the FBI standard for nearly one hundred years when agents used high-end technology like fountain pens and inkwells. For reasons without adequate explanation, the FBI keeps this practice despite the availability of much more reliable methods of documentation.

The 302 is woefully unreliable and extraordinarily powerful.

It's like a high-stakes game of "telephone" but with much, much bigger ramifications. An agent transcribes a subject's answers—again, by hand—and then using those notes and their memory records the interview on the 302. The length of the interview determines the length of the 302—it could be one hundred pages, it might be one. The person who was interviewed isn't allowed a peek, so there's no way of knowing whether their words were accurately documented. Unfortunately for them, whatever the agent puts in that 302 is considered the "official" record of what was said, which is bad news for anyone like Flynn who's interviewed by a corrupt agent like Strzok.

The FBI issued a memo in 2006 acknowledging there is no federal law requiring agents to electronically record interviews, and listed the reasons why the agency won't change its protocols. Among them:

- The presence of recording equipment could undermine the ability to establish rapport with the subject.
- Challenges by defendants in custody have been occasional and rarely successful.
- Not all recorded dialogue comes across as proper, and laypeople sometimes interpret it as a defendant's "involuntariness" and "misleading a defendant as to the quality of the evidence against him may appear to be unfair deceit."

What they're saying is they don't want recorded proof of an agent lying to someone about the evidence they have (or don't have), and that we "laypeople" are too simple-minded to understand tone and intent. Also, because only a few challenges have been successful, why bother to change?

However, the memo does stipulate there will be instances when prudence requires an interview be electronically recorded. One would think an interview with the national security advisor of the United States is one of those instances, but based on that 2006 memo, recording Flynn would have undermined the "rapport" Strzok and Pientka had with him—oh, and it would have made it difficult to falsify the 302, which is exactly what Strzok and his mistress, Lisa Page, would later do.

Consider the heinousness of that act. A senior level FBI agent and an FBI attorney together took the notes made by another agent who'd documented an interview with the national security advisor, then rewrote them to fit their predetermined narrative that Flynn had committed a crime. I've seen *The Shield*, and cops who do that end up in prison.

As we know, when the Flynn interview was over, Strzok and Pientka didn't believe Flynn was lying, and it's difficult to pull off a successful perjury trap if the subject doesn't perjure himself. Strzok and his mistress then took matters into their own hands.

The two were empowered to concoct a false record of how Flynn answered because his interview was conducted without a lawyer present. Remember when McCabe told Flynn he didn't need one because getting DOJ involved would just slow everything down? Typically, to interview an official at Flynn's level requires a request through the White House Counsel's office. Since this wasn't done with Flynn, there was no representative of that office present at the interview, which left Strzok and Page free to write anything they wanted in the 302.

It's an extraordinary act of lawlessness. This didn't just breach legal ethics, it obliterated them. What's even more heinous is the FBI kept this hidden for three years. It was only discovered because in late 2019, Flynn's legal team petitioned the court to toss Flynn's case "for outrageous government misconduct." It was, to use an oft-overused cliché, a "bombshell" revelation. Text messages between Strzok and Page revealed an incredible manipulation of the Flynn 302 with Strzok admitting to Page he was so heavily editing it that he was "trying not to completely re-write" it. It's exactly what a high school student would do when trying to pass off someone else's homework as their own. But a high school manipulation wouldn't send an innocent man to prison. What's worse is Page was helping edit the 302—she's not, nor has ever been, an FBI agent, and neither was she present for the Flynn interview.

Flynn's legal team has never laid eyes on the original version of the 302. The FBI claims it vanished. How convenient.

Page and Strzok would hammer away at the document, massaging and manipulating, writing, rewriting, and polishing repeatedly. A little more than two weeks had passed since Strzok and Pientka interviewed Flynn, and Strzok and Page were hard at work furiously crossing all the t's and dotting all the i's on their rewrite of Pientka's original 302. Strzok sent a copy of his version over to Page, and she wasn't pleased. Page texted back, "This document pisses me off. You didn't even attempt to make this cogent and readable? This is lazy work on your part." This was on February 10. Strzok's reply indicated he'd spent quite a bit of time reworking the 302: "Lisa, you didn't see it before my edits that went into what I sent you. I was 1) trying to completely rewrite the thing so as to save [Pientka's] voice and 2) get it out to you for general review and comment in anticipation of needing it soon." Here you have Strzok admitting that he's deliberately manipulating the document so others would think it was written by Pientka and not by him.

This behavior was so out of bounds it prompted a retired FBI special agent named Thomas Baker to submit an op-ed to *The Wall Street Journal* detailing how shocked he was. Baker pointed out how rewriting the Pientka notes wasn't even the most egregious thing Strzok did. Baker wrote, "Worse still, the FD-302 that was eventually provided to the court wasn't that of the agents' interview of Mr. Flynn. It was instead a FD-302 of an interview of *Mr. Strzok,* conducted months later, about his recollections of the original interview. Truly bizarre."[10]

It's true that nearly two years later at Flynn's sentencing in court (which we'll discuss in a bit) the 302 submitted wasn't the original—again, the original has conveniently vanished—and it wasn't Strzok's nor Pientka's. This 302 was written by *another* agent who'd interviewed Strzok six months after the Flynn interview, despite the fact that a 302 is required by FBI policy to be submitted within five working days of an interview.

Strzok's and Page's actions weren't merely bizarre: they were criminal. FBI officials whose sworn duty it is to uphold the tenets of the Constitution of the United States of America entered into a criminal conspiracy to frame someone. That's what happens when weaponizing the FBI for your own ends becomes more important than the pursuit of truth. Had the FBI long ago done away with the archaic practice of using handwritten notes and memory as the document of record, the Flynn charade likely would have ended before it even began.

CHAPTER 17

GUILTY

The plot against Flynn had become so outlandish it read like a French farce. While Strzok and his mistress, along with the complicit management of the FBI, executed the pièce de résistance of their "complot criminel," the Flynn case was strapped onto a runaway locomotive guided by a crazed engineer shoveling coal into an already overheated furnace. There was no stopping it.

By May 9, Trump had had about enough of Comey's shenanigans, and after recommendations from Attorney General Jeff Sessions and Deputy Attorney General Rod Rosenstein, he pulled the familiar catchphrase from his television show, *The Apprentice*, and told Comey, "You're fired." That same day Rosenstein issued a blistering two-and-a-half page memo calling out Comey's abhorrent behavior as FBI chief, such as:

- Refusing to accept that he'd made mistakes in the handling of the Clinton email investigation.
- That he was wrong to usurp the authority of the Attorney General and announce the Clinton email investigation should be closed without prosecution.
- Calling press conferences to gratuitously release "derogatory information about the subject of a declined criminal investigation."

Rosenstein accused Comey of harming the credibility of the FBI. At this point, he had no idea what Comey's FBI had done to Flynn. Imagine if he had. If Comey's tactless behavior with the Clinton email scandal harmed the credibility of the FBI and required his firing, what would his lawlessness in the Flynn matter have warranted? Public caning?

For all the illegalities of the Flynn case, and the role he played, it seems so anticlimactic that what brought down Comey was his poor handling of the investigation into Hillary Clinton's use of a private email server while she was secretary of state. It seems so, well, Al Capone-ish—a mob boss who wasn't imprisoned for murder but for tax evasion.

Trump tweeted how Comey had lost the confidence of almost everyone in Washington and that when things calmed down, "They will be thanking me!" He also promised that Comey would be replaced by someone who would do a far better job. His replacement was Christopher Wray, who was still on the job as this book went to print. The jury is still out on whether he was an improvement over Comey. But it was Comey's FBI predecessor who'd now be the one to carry the mantle for the Russian collusion investigation, which, of course, included the Flynn case. Eight days after Comey was fired, Rosenstein appointed Special Counsel Robert Mueller to take it over.

Mueller was eager to "get Trump," as we'd learn later, and he seemingly relished his new role. For two years, Mueller rolled up his sleeves and went to work tearing apart the country by pushing an investigation rooted in what he knew were falsehoods. He wanted Trump out of office and Flynn in jail. The goal was set, and the means to that end were inconsequential to him. Facts and truth gave way to gossip and lies. Mueller had no trepidation about ruining the lives of the innocent—especially if the innocent was a retired three-star Army general with ties to Trump. Once Mueller took over the collusion investigation, he and his mercenary investigators aggressively honed in on Flynn.

Flynn wouldn't fight Mueller alone. He retained two attorneys from the storied Washington, DC–based law firm of Covington & Burling—Robert Kelner and Steve Anthony. Kelner boasted a résumé that included successfully steering many cases through the treacherous waters of congressional investigations. He had a solid reputation amongst GOP circles. But Kelner was also a #NeverTrump-er, who'd once reportedly referred to Trump supporters as "zombies."[11] He was a curious choice considering the goal of Flynn's accusers was to destroy Trump's presidency.

Mueller did his part to help forward that goal, and he wasn't content to limit the scope of the Flynn investigation to just Michael. He also wanted his son, Michael Flynn Jr. A Virginia grand jury had been looking into the Flynn Intel Group's (FIG) dealings with Turkey—Flynn Jr. worked closely with his father at FIG and had also attended the now-infamous RT gala in Moscow. In June 2017, Mueller expanded his collusion investigation and assumed control of that grand jury investigation, too. Now, Junior was also in the crosshairs.

By the time the holidays arrived, Mueller had quite the gift for the elder Flynn. One week after Thanksgiving, on November 30, Mueller criminally charged him with making false statements to the FBI about the calls he'd had with Kislyak. The perjury trap laid by Bill Priestap, Comey, and McCabe had actually worked. At least for now, it did. The very next day, after having been charged with a crime, Flynn pleaded guilty.

Months before it came to this, Kelner had tried to secure an immunity deal for Flynn, where in exchange, he'd testify before Congress. Kelner's request was denied.

Though he never lied to Strzok nor Pientka nor Pence nor Trump about his call with Kislyak, Flynn told the court he had. It was a plea deal in which he'd admit guilt and cooperate with investigators, and, in turn, his sentence would be minimal—he was facing decades in prison. "My guilty plea and agreement to cooperate with the Special Counsel's Office reflect a decision I made in the best interests of my family and of our country," Flynn said afterward. "I accept full responsibility for my actions." But Flynn's admission was a lie. He'd lied about lying. Why? The feds made a hush-hush side deal with him—Flynn would plead guilty, and Mueller wouldn't file any charges against Michael Jr.

To get Flynn, the government strong-armed him by threatening his son. And his attorneys deemed their work a success? They did. Kelner and Anthony basked in the glow of the "Plea deal read round the world," as the headline trumpeted in *The American Lawyer*.[12] Incredibly, the magazine named them "litigators of the week" for the deal.

Covington & Burling billed Flynn roughly $5 million for their services. He was forced to sell his home and liquidate everything, and it still didn't make a dent in the due bill. For what? A coerced plea deal where he had to admit to doing something he didn't do to keep the federal government from ruining his son.

Yeah, some litigators.

The public would come to find out just how bad Flynn's legal representation had been when he dumped Kelner and Anthony and hired a new attorney—one who would blow the lid off of everything.

ACT 5

THE TIDE TURNS

CHAPTER 18

BRINGING IN A BIG GUN

FLYNN STAYED THE COURSE WITH COVINGTON & BURLING through the horrendous plea deal, several sentencing delays, his near bankruptcy from the legal fees, all of 2018, and about half of 2019.

During that time, Flynn was interviewed by DOJ lawyers and Mueller's team nineteen times—answering questions, providing documents, and generally cooperating with whatever they wanted to know about his work with the Trump team during the transition. Though we don't know just exactly what information Mueller gleaned from all of this, it was "substantial"[1] enough that he recommended Flynn's sentence not include jail time.

As the case appeared headed toward some sort of resolution—sentencing was all that remained—on March 24, 2019, Attorney General Bill Barr released the "principal conclusions" of Mueller's Russian collusion investigation. The report ignited a firestorm of "We told you so" from an exuberant Trump base as it concluded Mueller's investigation found absolutely no collusion, specifically that it "did not find that the Trump campaign, or anyone associated with it, conspired or coordinated" with Russian hackers to disrupt the 2016 presidential election "despite multiple offers from Russian-affiliated individuals to assist the Trump campaign."

The false narrative aimed at taking down Trump was falling apart like Chinese knockoff Louis Vuitton luggage.

Less than a month later, the DOJ released the full 448-page *Report on the Investigation into Russian Interference in the 2016 Presidential Election*, more commonly known as *The Mueller Report.* It officially confirmed what any citizen with even a modicum of sense already knew—there was no collusion between the Trump campaign and Russia. It also proved one other thing: Mueller wasted two years and more than $30 million of the taxpayers' money on a dishonest, partisan effort he and his cronies knew all along was built on a lie—a lie we now know was originated by Hillary Clinton to deflect from the investigation into her use of a private email server.

In late May of 2019, Mueller closed up shop and declared the collusion investigation officially closed. Eight days after that, Flynn officially pulled the trigger and fired Covington & Burling and their deal-making #NeverTrump attorneys, Kelner and Anthony. Flynn then made a move that later unleashed a legal blitzkrieg that would annihilate the criminal enterprise bent on destroying him.

On June 12, 2019, Flynn hired Sidney Powell as his attorney.

She was a big gun loaded for bear and, unlike Kelner and Anthony, was a vocal critic of Mueller. Powell—who was once a federal prosecutor—had zero tolerance for prosecutorial misconduct, and she knew Flynn's case was rife with it.

Powell's experience told her she faced quite a job ahead in untangling the mess of Flynn's entrapment and subsequent plea deal. The good news for Flynn? Powell was, and is, an expert in navigating the byzantine legal system to undo the gripping quagmires from which her clients think there is no escape.

She first branched out on her own in 1993 by leaving the comfort of a partnership in a large law firm to hang out her own shingle. For much of the last three decades, Powell has practiced appellate law and been lead counsel in more than five hundred appeals in the Fifth Circuit, although she also practices in the Second, Fourth, Ninth, Tenth, and Eleventh Circuit courts. In the appeals cases she's argued, Powell has had nearly 70 percent of them reversed. Given the Fifth Circuit's case-reversal rate of just 15 percent, her record is without equal—a Babe Ruthian level of success. Powell's playing chess while everyone else plays checkers. She might be a Southern belle originally from North Carolina and now settled in Dallas, but make no mistake, Powell is as pugnacious as she is brilliant. There was never a more perfect attorney for Michael Flynn.

Powell articulated her attitude toward shady prosecutors in a book she wrote in 2014 called *Licensed to Lie: Exposing Corruption in the Department of Justice.* It's a treatise on "the strong-arm, illegal, and unethical tactics used by headline-grabbing federal prosecutors in their narcissistic pursuit of power to the highest halls of our government," which was precisely what she now faced in the Flynn case.

Initially, after retaining Powell, Flynn continued to cooperate with the government and its collusion investigation, but by October 24, all bets were off. Powell filed a revealing thirty-seven-page powerhouse of a motion painting Mueller's investigation and the DOJ as corrupt forces and urged the court to "dismiss the entire prosecution for the outrageous and un-American misconduct of law enforcement officials." Powell rightfully cited the FBI's misleading 302s of Flynn's interview, which we now know were rewritten by Strzok and his mistress. Powell also argued prosecutors withheld exculpatory information or were late in providing it. "Exculpatory" comes from the Medieval Latin word "exculpatus," which translates as "freed from blame." Clearly, exculpatory information would have been helpful to Flynn's defense since he was free from blame. Powell had issued an ultimatum—hand over ALL the evidence or drop the case.

She was on the offensive—a tactic foreign to Flynn's previous counsel, which had been all too eager to raise a white flag and put him into a bad plea deal. Powell brought up how the FBI orchestrated the ambush interview "not for the purpose of discovering any evidence of criminal activity—they already had tapes of all the relevant conversations about which they questioned Mr. Flynn—but for the purpose of trapping him into making statements they could allege as false." This is the first time we heard so starkly about the perjury trap the FBI had set for Flynn.

Powell ran through the litany of defects in the feds' behavior: how McCabe advised Flynn to forego legal counsel; that the FBI agents rehearsed their tactics to keep Flynn "relaxed" and "unguarded" so he wouldn't know the significance of the conversation; and the "anxious text messages between Agent Strzok and his paramour, Lisa Page—McCabe's Special Counsel—disclosing the deep personal involvement of these officials and others in an enterprise without a legitimate law enforcement objective." The motion was an iron-to-the-face list of everything wrong with the Flynn case. "When the Director of the FBI, and a group of his close associates, plot to set up an innocent man and create a crime, while taking affirmative steps to ensnare him by refusing to follow procedures designed to prevent such inadvertent missteps," Powell wrote, "this amounts to conduct so shocking to the conscience and so inimical to our system of justice that it requires the dismissal of the charges for outrageous government conduct."

Powell wasn't content to let federal prosecutors run unchecked over her client. She hammered at the DOJ's refusal to turn over the exculpatory evidence proving Flynn was framed. Even back in 2018, long before Flynn had hired Powell, Judge Emmet Sullivan ordered Mueller to hand it all over to Covington & Burling, the previous defense team. He didn't. Powell had been watching the case and wrote an op-ed accusing Mueller of "thumbing his nose at Judge Sullivan's order," and said the evidence suggested Mueller "destroyed or suppressed evidence, and obstructed justice."[2]

Fast-forward a year, and now it was Powell and not Covington & Burling trying to get prosecutors to hand over the exculpatory evidence, but this time Sullivan, revealing his bias, denied her request to order them to do so. (More on Sullivan later.) In a ninety-two-page summary of his decision to reject Powell's request, Sullivan contended that Flynn forfeited his basic constitutional rights under the Fourth Amendment by pleading guilty in the first place. He further argued that even if Flynn hadn't given up his Fourth Amendment rights, he would have had to establish that the exculpatory information he requested be "favorable" to his defense for him to be allowed to have it.

Wait—what?

That's the requirement under the Brady Rule, which requires prosecutors to disclose exculpatory evidence to the defense, including evidence rebutting the accused's guilt. The rule is named after 1963's *Brady v. Maryland*, which held that the government's withholding of evidence material to the determination of either guilt or punishment of a criminal defendant violates the defendant's constitutional right to due process. However, Brady puts the burden of proof on the *defense* to show the outcome of the trial would have been different had the prosecutor disclosed that evidence. Sullivan claimed that Flynn failed to establish the outcome would have been different. What actually was established—at least with his response—was that Sullivan was a willing participant in the plan to subvert Flynn because any first-year law student with just a morsel of brain tissue would have been able to surmise the evidence provided in Powell's motion proved the government had railroaded Flynn.

As Powell had noted a month earlier, "There never would have been a plea to begin with if the government had met its Brady obligation."[3]

To summarize—Flynn, who'd been coerced by threats against his son into pleading guilty to something he didn't do, lost his constitutional rights because he'd been coerced by threats against his son into pleading guilty to something he didn't do.

Powell would soon fix that.

CHAPTER 19

I PLEADED "GUILTY." YEAH ABOUT THAT...

As 2020 dawned, the hits just kept on comin' for Flynn. On January 7, federal prosecutors showed their true colors and took back the recommendation they'd made that Flynn serve no prison time—they now asked that he serve up to six months. They claimed he abused their trust, refused to accept responsibility for what he'd done, and wouldn't help them prosecute his FIG business partner, Bijan Rafiekian. Truth is, they were pissed—pissed that Flynn was now fighting back. He no longer had representation that would say, "Thank you, sir, may I have another?" every time a fed paddle-swatted him on the back of his tighty-whities.

Powell could play that way, too. Exactly one week later, she filed a motion to withdraw Flynn's guilty plea.

She accused the prosecutors of bad faith and vindictiveness and of violating their end of Flynn's plea deal. The motion spelled it out. Powell argued they'd engaged in "pure retaliation" against Flynn ever since he'd hired new counsel. "This can only be because with new, unconflicted counsel, Mr. Flynn refused to lie for the prosecution," she wrote.

Game on.

Powell's growing ire took further aim at the government when she filed more motions within days of that first one. On January 29, she filed two—one citing "egregious government conduct," and the other, a real bunker buster, accusing Flynn's previous law firm, Covington & Burling, of conflict of interest and ineffective assistance of counsel.

Prosecutors then argued Flynn's former attorneys, Kelner and Anthony, should testify due to Flynn's claims of ineffective assistance. In a motion filed on February 9, they wrote, "The government requests that the Court suspend the current briefing schedule...until such time as the government has been able to confer with Covington regarding the information it seeks." They also asked Sullivan to order Flynn to waive his attorney-client privileges with Covington & Burling.

There was so much going on, Sullivan postponed Flynn's sentencing indefinitely.

The next couple of months would see Attorney General William Barr bring in an outside prosecutor named Jeff Jensen, a U.S. attorney from the Eastern District of Missouri, to review Flynn's case, alongside Flynn's primary prosecutor, Brandon Van Grack.

Out of that came the mother of all bombs, one that annihilated everything.

On April 29, the DOJ turned over exculpatory documents: the handwritten notes by the FBI's former head of counterintelligence Bill Priestap. Remember the ones documenting the now-infamous meeting with Comey and McCabe where Priestap asked, "What's our goal? Truth, admission or to get him to lie so we can prosecute him or get him fired?" Then they decided if that didn't work, "we get him to admit to breaking the Logan Act, give facts to DOJ and have them decide."

This was more than a smoking gun. This was DNA, fingerprints, and a bloody glove.

Powell exploded when she read Priestap's notes. "I can't even tell you how outraged I am!" she told Sean Hannity on Fox News.[4] "It's just absolutely appalling what these agents, and then special counsel operatives, did to General Flynn. It's abuse of their authority at every turn. I interpret the notes as absolutely damning of their conduct and their plan."

This indeed was the damning proof that the Flynn case had been a setup from the beginning.

A little more than a week after that revelation, on May 7, came a stunning turn of events—the DOJ announced it was dropping the case.

There was little reason to move forward. It was now so publicly and painfully clear Flynn had been set up and hadn't done anything worthy of prosecution. Even the DOJ's motion to dismiss contained several Captain Obvious–esque statements most any sensible person already knew, such as, "…continued prosecution of this case would not serve the interests of justice." Ya think? The facts of the case showed Flynn committed no crime. DOJ also found there was never any basis for the FBI to question Flynn at the White House that fateful January day in 2017. Oh, and the lie prosecutors claimed he told to Strzok and Pientka during their interview about sanctions? The motion pointed out, "Mr. Flynn pleaded guilty to making false statements that were not 'material' to any investigation."

The DOJ made clear it had no interest in penalizing someone for a crime when they weren't sure there even was a crime—or if Flynn had committed one, they didn't believe it could be proven "beyond a reasonable doubt."

The filing revealed a distinct lack of basis for any charge and took apart, piece by piece, every aspect of the feds' case. So complete was the dismantling of the bogus prosecution one had to wonder if the case would have made it this far if not for the corrupt actions of Comey's FBI and the rubber stamp provided by the equally corrupt Robert Mueller. And not coincidentally, the lead prosecutor, Brandon Van Grack, withdrew from the Flynn case, without explanation, the same day the DOJ filed the motion to dismiss. He knew what was coming. Van Grack was the wretched lawyer who'd threatened Flynn's son and strong-armed Flynn into pleading guilty in the first place.

As the DOJ reviewed Flynn's case, they'd sent Powell more of the exculpatory evidence she'd been demanding from prosecutors—notes and internal emails that proved the FBI's intention to frame Flynn. They were more eye-opening than even she'd imagined. "The revelations of corruption by the FBI to intentionally frame General Flynn for crimes the FBI manufactured piles on with each new production of documents," she said in a statement at the time. Little did she know of the trove of even more damning notes still to come.

Even the president, more than three years after Flynn's forced resignation as national security advisor, called it as he saw it in his own inimitable way: "They came at him with 15 buses and he's standing in the middle of the highway. What they did to this man," Trump told a group at a White House event. "They tormented him. They destroyed him. But he's going to come back."

Flynn had won! It was over!

Or was it?

As Flynn and Powell would soon learn, Judge Sullivan had other plans.

CHAPTER 20

JURIST? MORE LIKE AN ACTIVIST

When the DOJ filed its motion to dismiss the charges against Flynn and to drop the case entirely, Flynn, Flynn's family, his supporters, and Powell were ecstatic. How couldn't they be? The nightmare that had lasted for more than three years was over. Though it came at a great cost, Powell was able to prove Flynn's innocence and that he'd been the victim of a lawless government frame job that came all the way from the Oval Office. All he needed was the presiding judge to affirm the dismissal, which happens in almost every case, nay, in *every* case. After all, a judge isn't a prosecutor. A judge doesn't have standing in the case. A judge isn't a party in the case. A judge is objective and independent.

Unless it's Judge Emmet Sullivan.

He refused to affirm the dismissal. In what may be a first in the modern age of American jurisprudence, a U.S. district court judge unilaterally decided that prosecutors dropping the charges should be ignored and then made himself a party in the case for which he was the assigned jurist. More simply stated, after the DOJ dropped the charges against Flynn, Sullivan picked up the case, pursued the charges, and took steps to take it to trial.

The absurdity reads like a bad episode of *Boston Legal.*

Sullivan claimed he had the right to decide whether the dropping of the charges was a veiled, politically motivated attempt by the DOJ to help a friend of Trump.

No, he didn't.

That's not how this works. That's not how any of this works.

A federal district court judge has absolutely no authority whatsoever over prosecutorial decisions. That's a function of the executive branch, not the judicial. Sullivan had zero legal authority to move forward with prosecuting this case.

Conservative radio icon Rush Limbaugh may have summed it up most succinctly: "I've never heard of a judge being allowed to become a participant in a case when the prosecutors have dropped it."

The irony in Sullivan's assertion is that it isn't the DOJ making politically motivated decisions—it's him.

Powell called Sullivan's actions "irregular to the point of being eccentric."

To advance the case, Sullivan appointed another judge as amicus curiae, which means "friend of the court," to present arguments opposing the DOJ's motion to dismiss. The judge he appointed was a former federal judge, a Trump critic, named John Gleeson who would also argue Sullivan's other point—that Flynn be charged additionally with contempt and perjury. They wanted Flynn charged for lying about lying when he pleaded guilty.

Does this sound more like an objective jurist or a prosecutor?

Fact is, Sullivan isn't a jurist, he's a biased activist.

During one of Flynn's earlier hearings, back in December 2018, Sullivan berated Flynn, implying he'd committed treason after falsely accusing him of being an unregistered agent of a foreign country while serving as national security advisor. That was a lie, and so absurd even the government's lawyers went to Flynn's defense. They informed Sullivan he'd not represented a foreign government while serving as national security advisor. To be fair, though, Flynn's firm did represent Turkey *before* he took the job at the White House.

Nonetheless, Sullivan publicly slandered a decorated, three-star Army general who fought to end the spread of communism and terrorism, saying he "undermines everything this flag over here stands for." Truthfully, what undermines the American flag is a rogue judge showing contempt for the Constitution of the United States of America, pushing a political agenda from the bench, and disrespectfully defaming an Army war veteran in open court.

Sullivan's "friend of the court," Gleeson, didn't hide his disdain for Flynn either. In an op-ed he co-wrote for *The Washington Post* titled, "The Flynn Case Isn't Over Until the Judge Says It's Over," he mirrored Sullivan's accusation that the DOJ's decision to drop the case wasn't motivated so much by the law, but by politics. "There has been nothing regular about the department's effort to dismiss the Flynn case. The record reeks of improper political influence," he wrote. Clearly, Gleeson had no objectivity. Here he suggests the DOJ was being influenced, likely by Trump, and that Flynn's case should continue. "The Justice Department's move to dismiss the prosecution of former national security adviser Michael Flynn does not need to be the end of the case—and it shouldn't be." Gleeson further suggested that prosecutors abused their power, and if the court approved their request for dismissal, it would make the court "a party to corruption."[5]

The op-ed was Gleeson's valiant effort at sullying the DOJ with accusations their decision to drop the Flynn case was politically motivated, but in reality, as we said earlier, the only politically motivated decision in this entire sordid situation was Sullivan's.

Gleeson filed a brief asking that the DOJ's motion to dismiss be denied, and he requested Flynn be sent to jail. In the irony of ironies, Gleeson accused the government of "misconduct" for requesting the dismissal. As we know, it was the government's misconduct in the first place that led to Flynn's guilty plea. Gleeson also wanted four weeks to make his arguments to the court, then more time on top of that to allow the defense or the DOJ to reply to his arguments, and then even more time beyond that to allow him to file his replies to the replies, and then he wanted to schedule oral arguments after all of that. This would have dragged on for months.

Most conservatives could easily see through Sullivan's and Gleeson's biased motivation. Sean Davis, co-founder of *The Federalist*, pretty well summed up their feelings about Sullivan's refusal to drop the case and his appointment of Gleeson as the "friend of the court." On Twitter, Davis wrote, "Judge Emmet G. Sullivan just signaled he's not interested in the law, due process, equal rights, or justice. He already called Flynn a traitor in open court, and now he's going to invite left-wing lawyers write his final order against Flynn for him."

It's also difficult to assume Sullivan could be unbiased toward Flynn when he's friends with the man who helped set him up—James Comey, whom Sullivan reportedly helped secure a $100,000 payday for a twelve-minute speech at Howard University, Sullivan's alma mater.

After Sullivan's refusal to affirm the dismissal and his appointment of an amicus curiae, a week later, Powell filed an emergency petition with the U.S. Court of Appeals for the DC Circuit to order Sullivan to grant the DOJ's motion to dismiss the case, vacate its order appointing amicus curiae or "friend of court," and reassign the case to a different judge. She cited the separation of powers and how Sullivan's court had disregarded the constitutional imperative that gives the power to prosecute solely to the executive branch. Powell laid it out:

- The district court has no authority to adopt the prosecutor's role or change the issues in the case by inviting or appointing amici to perform the investigation or prosecution that the court deems appropriate.
- The district court order appointing an amicus is both unauthorized and bespeaks a disturbing lack of appreciation of the court's limited role when confronted with a motion to dismiss by the government in a criminal case.

"The district judge in this case has abandoned any pretense of being an objective umpire. He wants to pitch, bat, run bases, and play shortstop. In truth, he is way out in left field," Powell said, stating the obvious about Sullivan in the petition.

The same day Powell filed her emergency petition, Sullivan issued a scheduling order further delaying the case along by setting the start of oral arguments for nearly two months later: July 16. In her motion, Powell accused Sullivan of dragging out the case on purpose: "The district judge's orders reveal his plan to continue the case indefinitely, rubbing salt in General Flynn's open wound from the Government's misconduct and threatening him with criminal contempt."

Given Sullivan's bias, it's obvious his goal was to prolong the process for as long as possible, at least through the 2020 presidential election with the hopes of a Biden victory, which would mean a new attorney general—one that would rescind the DOJ's motion to dismiss and ultimately send Flynn to prison.

The appeals court gave Sullivan ten days to respond, and he did by hiring a high-powered, well-connected attorney named Beth Wilkinson—the wife of CNN political analyst David Gregory—who'd also lent her expertise to now-Supreme Court Justice Brett Kavanaugh during his confirmation hearing, and to former Hillary Clinton staffers during the infamous email and private server scandal.

Wilkinson's first move in the case was to wait the ten days and then file a response telling the appeals court to "holster" the "potent" weapon of a mandamus (court order) and let Sullivan evaluate Flynn's request.

Telling a federal appeals court panel to basically piss off is certainly an interesting strategy. As *Dodgeball's* Pepper Brooks famously said, "It's a bold strategy, Cotton. Let's see if it pays off for them."

It had now been nearly a month since the DOJ dropped Flynn's case, and not only was he still twisting in the wind, but Sullivan, through his attorney, displayed the unmitigated chutzpah to tell judges from the U.S. Court of Appeals for the DC Circuit to stay out of his business.

It didn't work.

The court rendered its decision and on June 24, in a stunning slap back to a defiant judge, ordered Sullivan to grant the DOJ's request to dismiss the charges against Flynn, and to boot, vacated Sullivan's order to appoint a "friend of the court."

Game. Set. Match.

The two-to-one decision by the three-member panel thoroughly lashed Sullivan for what the court called his "unprecedented intrusions on individual liberty and the Executive's charging authority." It also left no ambiguity that Sullivan never had the authority to push the case forward. "It is about whether, after the government has explained why a prosecution is no longer in the public interest, the district judge may prolong the prosecution by appointing an amicus, encouraging public participation, and probing the government's motives. On that, both the Constitution and cases are clear: he may not."

He. May. Not.

The news reverberated across Washington, and once Trump heard it he sent out a congratulatory message on Twitter: "Great! Appeals Court Upholds Justice Department's Request To Drop Criminal Case Against General Michael Flynn!"

The lone dissenter on the court panel was Judge Robert Wilkins, who'd, of course, been appointed by Obama. The other two who sided with Flynn were appointed by conservatives—Judge Neomi Rao was a Trump appointee, and Judge Karen Henderson had been appointed by George W. Bush.

The victory was sweet, but as we'd seen time and again, it was short-lived. Sullivan refused to abide by the order and instead fought it by requesting an en banc hearing on the issue. An en banc hearing is one where the full court rather than just a panel hears the arguments. After considering the issue, the appeals court ultimately decided it would, in fact, grant Sullivan's request, and it vacated its own order. The court set yet another date where the full court would rehear arguments. At this point, the Flynn case was a hamster on a wheel.

The only certain thing in the case was that nothing was certain.

The lingering impasse between Flynn and Sullivan would be decided by the full appeals court of eleven judges on August 11. It's quite the feat when a judge in a case, as Sullivan did here, manages to get both the prosecution and the defendant on the same team.

The inconceivable legal saga would never have gotten this far if not for one judge with a politically motivated axe to grind—a judge who believed an ally of Trump was getting off without consequence. It really was quite extraordinary.

When August 11 arrived, the full court seemed unlikely to issue the same ruling its three-judge panel had. Powell and the DOJ attorneys were made to answer strident questions about why they believed the court should intervene, especially given that Sullivan had only delayed the case and not actually ruled on it.

The court took nearly three weeks to render a judgment, and when it did, all anyone who supported Flynn could do was shake their head. Incredibly, the appeals court rejected Flynn's request to compel Sullivan to approve the DOJ's motion to dismiss the case and sent it back to Sullivan.

In its decision, the court determined Flynn hadn't shown he had "no other adequate means to attain the relief he desires." It also refused to reassign the case from Sullivan to another judge, saying Flynn hadn't proven a "clear and indisputable right to reassignment."

That was quite the kick in the kisser, and the best was yet to come.

The very next day, Sullivan ordered Flynn, the DOJ, and his "friend of the court," Judge Gleeson, to bring a proposed schedule for the presentation of oral and written arguments within three weeks. But by the next hearing before

Sullivan—held virtually on September 29 due to COVID-19 safety protocols—Powell had had it. She demanded Sullivan recuse himself. And the two engaged in a fiery exchange.

"It's absolutely unprecedented for proceedings against a defendant to be conducted by a person who actively litigated against him," Powell charged. She wanted him off the case and for good reason. The conflict of interest here was truly unprecedented. Would any person of sound mind believe Sullivan could now be an impartial jurist?

The two argued back and forth, often interrupting each other. Powell would demand recusal, Sullivan would challenge her to file a motion. Though not a word-for-word actual transcription, their exchanges sounded something like this—

"Recuse yourself!"

"Well, file a motion then."

"I will."

"Fine."

"Then do it already."

"Oh, I am."

"You could have filed one, but you didn't."

"Yeah, well, here's why I waited."

"I don't want to hear anymore!"

Sullivan gave Powell a week to file the motion requesting his recusal. Powell did just that, and boy, did she ever.

On October 1, she filed the formal "Motion to Disqualify Judge Emmet Sullivan"—a forty-page slash-and-burn opus.

Powell was clearly tired of Sullivan's games, and she laid out the case succinctly, albeit passionately.

"Judge Sullivan's Prejudicial Statements and Conduct Have Become Increasingly Shrill, Unprecedented, and Prejudicial and Apparently Influenced by Extra-Judicial Sources," Powell headlined one section. In it, she cited Sullivan's contemptuous remarks at the sentencing hearing when Sullivan "expressed his 'disdain' and 'disgust' for General Flynn's conduct, stated that he 'sold his country out,' and suggested that General Flynn had committed 'treason.'" Powell claimed Sullivan stole those lines from *The Rachel Maddow Show* on MSNBC that had aired the night before the hearing. During that episode, Maddow, according to Powell, "made the charge that General Flynn 'sold his country out' and 'was a national security advisor to a presidential candidate who was secretly also a foreign agent' for the Turkish government."

Among Powell's assertions:

- Sullivan read Gleeson's op-ed in *The Washington Post* and then adopted the procedure Gleeson recommended within it to "delay and derail the government's motion to dismiss." Within the op-ed Gleeson did call for Sullivan to deny the DOJ's request to dismiss the case. Powell pointed out Sullivan then hired Gleeson within forty-eight hours of the op-ed's appearance in the paper. "This cake was already baked when Gleeson first laid out his ingredients in the opinion piece well before Judge Sullivan put it in the oven two days later," Powell wrote.

- "Statutes require a judge to disqualify himself when 'he is a party to the proceeding,' which Sullivan was. "When the district judge aggressively petitioned for rehearing en banc as if he were a party, it invoked the application of this section sufficiently to trigger the application of the appearance of bias and for personal bias against General Flynn himself."
- "Judge Sullivan became an accuser in this case no later than when he sought charges against General Flynn for perjury or contempt, and it is a violation of General Flynn's due process right for him to remain the judge."
- "The circumstances of this case lead any reasonable observer to believe that the current judge has a personal interest in the outcome, is irreparably biased against General Flynn, and is actively litigating against him."
- "Never has a court worked so hard or stretched the facts and law so far to smear a defendant and his counsel—and to try to deny an undeniable motion to dismiss."

Powell claimed Sullivan's "continued presence in the case has become a national scandal" that undermined the public's confidence in the federal judiciary's ability to be impartial and threatened faith in the rule of law.

Then Powell drove it home, formally demanding Sullivan's disqualification. "Judge Sullivan's increasingly hostile and unprecedented words and deeds in what has become his own prosecution of General Flynn mandate his disqualification from further participation in these proceedings and the referral of his conduct to the D.C. Circuit Judicial Council."

The motion was an impassioned plea, and its arguments compelling. Powell made a near irrefutable case that Sullivan was irreparably biased against Flynn. But at the end of the day, would it matter? As we've mentioned, one of Sullivan's clear goals was to delay the case beyond Election Day 2020 in the hopes that Joe Biden would be president, and a new attorney general would reimpose the case against Flynn. He was so motivated to drag out the case that a week and a half before Election Day, Sullivan pulled one of the most absurd rulings from his bag of increasingly asinine tricks. He ordered the DOJ to prove the documents submitted in its filing to drop the charges against Flynn weren't doctored. At that point, the whole thing had become a meme.

Sullivan's intentions were so patently absurd, it was comical. Typically, judges take DOJ filings at face value. The man simply would not let it go.

In his ruling, Sullivan said, "...the government has not provided a declaration attesting that the Exhibits are true and correct copies." Too bad that same standard wasn't applied to the information in the bogus Steele Dossier.

Ultimately, Sullivan did achieve his goal of dragging the case beyond Election Day, however, as he'd soon learn, the notion that a Biden win would seal Flynn's fate was supremely foolish.

CHAPTER 21

PARDON ME

When the sun came over the horizon on November 4th, 2020, Flynn's situation could not have looked more dire. It was the morning after Election Day and most of the country was still punch-drunk from the relentless blunt force of horrid election coverage delivered by partisan activists disguised as journalists, cocksure pundits offering analysis on par with a high school civics class, and networks calling states before their polls had even closed. Once the fog lifted it was clear that several states played a Three-card Monte sleight of hand with the ballots making it appear Biden had won the presidency, which meant Flynn was still on the hook—exactly what Sullivan had wanted.

What was Powell to do? She pivoted from the Flynn case to challenging the presidential election results. Powell went to work fulltime pursuing legal remedies to what was now obvious election fraud in key battleground states. She wasn't doing this for Flynn, she was doing it for the country, though Flynn would certainly benefit if Biden wasn't the president. Remember, it was Biden who helped orchestrate Flynn's takedown by suggesting he be prosecuted under the Logan Act.

The days and the weeks went by. The election was being challenged. Powell announced she'd soon "release the Kraken." Flynn wasn't being discussed, he wasn't in the news, and all he and his family could do was wait. A man whose case was dropped by the DOJ six months earlier still had no closure thanks to one corrupt, activist judge, and now, a corrupt election.

By Wednesday, November 25th, after three weeks of nonstop partisan rancor, Americans were in desperate need of respite from election overload. On that day most normal people just wanted to think about turkey, stuffing (yes, it's stuffing, not "dressing"), pumpkin pie, nog, and whether pandemic restrictions instituted by totalitarian governors would ruin Thanksgiving the next day. Then at 3:08 pm, before the first sleigh went over the river and through the woods, an announcement appeared on Twitter that gave Flynn something for which he'd be very, very thankful—

> "It is my Great Honor to announce that General Michael T. Flynn has been granted a Full Pardon.

> Congratulations to @GenFlynn and his wonderful family, I know you will now have a truly fantastic Thanksgiving!"

President Trump had granted Flynn a full pardon, and it was the greatest gift he could have ever received, though it was somewhat bittersweet—Flynn and Powell had hoped he'd be exonerated in a court of law, have the case dismissed, and not need a pardon. Nevertheless, on Thanksgiving Day, Flynn issued a personal statement that expressed not just his thanks, but his relief—

> "By Almighty God's grace and with the love and courage of my wife Lori, the strength and fortitude of our families, and the inspiration of our friends and every single patriot who circled me with their prayers, wisdom, and kindness, I say thank you from the bottom of my heart. For the first time in more than four years and because of my fearless attorney, Sidney Powell, the Guardian Angel of American Justice, and thousands of good people with endless energy rallying together on my behalf, I breathe freedom and liberty today."

Trump made sure he covered everything in Flynn's pardon—the original charge of making a false statement to the FBI and the ensuing guilty plea, all of the Mueller investigation, including any grand jury proceedings conducted by the Special Counsel, and the bogus perjury charge Sullivan had threatened.

The DOJ filed the pardon three years to the day that Flynn signed the horrid plea deal his original attorneys made with prosecutors—the one where he lied about lying so they'd leave his son alone.

Flynn was finally free. Or was he?

Following the pardon, there'd been indications Sullivan would continue to push the case, further politicizing it by possibly claiming the language in the pardon was too broad. This notion wasn't that outlandish given Sullivan's doggedness in his bias. One day went by, then another, then another, then a week, then a few more days. Nothing from the bench.

Sullivan let Flynn twist for another 13 days.

Finally, on December 8th, holding a bad hand and with no chips left to play, Sullivan folded.

"Sore loser" doesn't come close to adequately describing Sullivan's behavior in dismissing the case. He did, in fact, dismiss it but he did so in a whiny 43-page commentary in which he took parting shots at Flynn, Trump, Attorney General William Barr, and the DOJ. Sadly for Sullivan, his foot-stomping dissertation revealed more about him than it did any of them.

If there'd been any doubts about his bias, this settled them.

Sullivan admitted he planned to deny the DOJ's request to dismiss the case. He described their rationale for dropping it as "dubious" and said that just because Flynn was pardoned didn't mean he's innocent. Sullivan discounted all of the evidence proving Flynn had been set up, and accused Trump of showing favoritism. Then he rolled out a two-ton boulder of irony, "President Trump's decision to pardon Mr. Flynn is a political decision, not a legal one." Was Sullivan sporting a straight face when he wrote that? If anyone had been making political decisions rather than legal ones it was him.

In the end, Sullivan had to recognize he'd been trumped, "Because the law recognizes the President's political power to pardon, the appropriate course is to dismiss this case as moot," he wrote.

The peevishness of Sullivan's opinion was summarized best by Senator Tom Cotton who, after reading it, wrote on Twitter, "This opinion reads like the delusional ramblings of a Resistance lawyer afflicted with Trump Derangement Syndrome. Judge Sullivan has demonstrated blatant bias and injudicious temperament throughout this case. He has no business remaining on the federal bench."

Just what was Sullivan's motivation? What was the point of his political crusade? Was he just a bitter Obama appointee with, as Senator Cotton described, Trump Derangement Syndrome?

Whatever the reason, Sullivan's transparent charade should never, have ever, gone on for so long.

CHAPTER 22

SULLIVAN'S UNINTENDED GIFT

THE CAVEAT TO ALL OF THIS IS IF SULLIVAN HAD NOT INSISTED on pushing his agenda and dragging out the case, we likely never would have had the explosive revelations of the host of improprieties and, well, sketchy FBI behavior in their efforts to destroy Flynn.

Attached to one of Powell's incendiary filings in late September were the transcripts of text messages between FBI agents that were so outlandish, at first read, it was hard to believe they were real.

Agents were so worried about the FBI's potentially illegal behavior during the collusion investigation, which included

Flynn, they bought liability insurance to protect themselves in the event they were sued.

Just a week and a half before Trump took office, the text messages dated January 10, 2017, reveal a flurry of activity like roaches running for cover when the lights come on.

> "We all went and purchased professional liability insurance."
>
> "Holy crap! All the analysts too?"
>
> "Yep. All the folks at the Agency as well."
>
> "That really, really sucks."
>
> "The whole thing is pretty ugly. We shall see how things pan out."
>
> "Can I ask who are the most likely litigators? As far as potentially suing y'all."
>
> "Haha, who knows…I think the concern when we got it was that there was a big leak at DOJ and the NYT among others was going to do a piece."

The piece was the story leaked to the *The New York Times* of the briefing at Trump Tower and the existence of the Steele Dossier.

The notes between FBI agents also showed an overarching infatuation by the higher-ups with conspiracy theories rather than actual evidence and a concern about what would happen if anyone starting poking around what they'd been doing. "I'm tellying (sic) man, if this thing ever gets FOIA'd, there are going to be some tough questions asked," one of the agents wrote.

If agents were so concerned about being sued for the underhanded tactics they'd been using to smear Trump and Flynn, Page, Papadopoulos, Manafort, and the rest, then it implies the corruption within the FBI wasn't systemic but rather dictated by its leadership. Not every agent inside the bureau was engaged in insidious, contemptible behavior.

One agent in particular, assigned to the Flynn investigation, seemed one of the good guys—an agent named William Barnett. Just a day after the text messages revealing the liability insurance purchases, a transcript emerged of his interview with DOJ prosecutors, and if there was ever a "bombshell," he fired it.

Barnett told them Flynn's case was "opaque" and lacked specific evidence that any crimes had been committed—he didn't see any wrongdoing. He thought Flynn's trip to Moscow for the RT gala was ill-advised but certainly not illegal. Barnett also felt he was on a bit of a fishing expedition with both the Flynn and Russian collusion investigations because there wasn't a specific criminal allegation, which lends weight to the idea the feds had embraced the mantra of the head of the Soviet Union's secret police, Lavrentiy Beria: "Show me the man and I'll show you the crime." The FBI was in search of a crime.

Barnett also believed an attorney for the Special Counsel Office was "obsessed" with Flynn and Russia. He believed she had an agenda.

In the very last line of his interview was the one nugget that opened up everything. It was a big one—Barnett said Flynn's prosecution was being used by Robert Mueller and his team as a means to "get Trump."

And there it is. Three years and tens of millions of dollars, countless lives destroyed, and a three-star general dragged through a nearly four-year legal fight all because Mueller and his band of rogues wanted to "get Trump."

EPILOGUE

CHAPTER 23

WHY YOU SHOULD CARE

Lieutenant General Michael T. Flynn (Ret.) is the victim of one of the most blatant perversions of justice in the history of the United States of America. A man who spent nearly all of his adult life in the service of his country fell victim to an organized plot orchestrated by the very government for which he'd served—prey for bloodthirsty political animals determined to devour him. Flynn committed no crimes. Yet, he's been tormented by unscrupulous people devoid of decency, threatened with prison, lied to, and framed—and ground like grist for the mill.

We know now the evil cast upon this innocent man was summoned from the Oval Office and the J. Edgar Hoover

Building. The president, vice president, FBI brass, intelligence chiefs, crooked agents, lawyers, one biased judge, and his "friend of the court" all worked in tandem to ruin one man. Why? Because they hate America and everything she stands for.

And they hate you.

One might stop and say, "Hold on, don't you think that's an exaggeration? It's just Donald Trump they hated. That's why those bad actors tried to ruin him and his associates." But one would be wrong. The goal of the criminal Deep State conspirators wasn't just to ruin Trump; it was to ruin his presidency, and that's how you know they hate America. You see, free and fair elections are the cornerstones of our Republic. Men and women fought and died to ensure that right. Donald Trump was the duly elected president of the United States—to conspire to tear down his presidency, or that of any president, is to conspire to tear at the very fabric of America. That isn't something a person who loves America would, or could, do.

The United States is engaged in a civil war for its soul. It's law-abiding versus law-breaking. It's good versus evil. It's freedom versus oppression. When the pillars of our Republic are pulled down from within by the very people the citizens entrust with their care, those people must be stopped. America is a shining city upon a hill whose beacon light guides freedom-loving people everywhere. Ronald Reagan said that.

He was right. And freedom-loving people must fight for it. An America that allows subversion from the FBI or any branch of the government; an America that allows a failed presidential candidate to make up allegations to frame a president as an agent of Russia; an America that allows government officials to unfairly target the innocent, to frame them, lead them into perjury traps, threaten their children, drag them through the courts, and bankrupt them, isn't America at all.

"The only thing necessary for the triumph of evil is that good men should do nothing," said eighteenth-century statesman and philosopher Edmund Burke, a man considered the father of modern conservatism. And we need heroes who'll stand up and do something.

The real hero of this story, the titan to whom all Americans owe a debt of gratitude, is the tenacious woman who heroically exposed the underbelly of evil rooted deep within the halls of Washington. If not for Sidney Powell and her legal brilliance, the crooked system that ran roughshod over Flynn might never have been tempered.

Much of what we know about the shady and oft-criminal behavior of Comey, Mueller, McCabe, Obama, Biden, Strzok, and the rest of the Deep State miscreants resulted from Powell's fortitude and drive—oh, and likely a team of damn fine researchers.

The Flynn case matters because America is exceptional. America has a special calling and a divine purpose. In

America, we embrace our exceptionalism, and it's difficult to be exceptional if we allow the bad seeds in government to destroy the country from within.

America is a nation of laws, and no one should be above them. As former U.S. Representative John Linder of Georgia once wrote, "When a nation's laws are flouted by the political leadership it is only a matter of time until the populace shows the same disrespect for law and order."[1] If America's political leadership can frame a decorated three-star general, drag him through the courts, and destroy his livelihood for years, imagine what it can do to you.

We've got to be vigilant and strong. As a country, we can never allow what the Deep State did to Flynn to happen to anyone else.

When U.S. Attorney for Connecticut John Durham began looking into the origins of the Russian collusion investigation and reviewed the Flynn case files, he, like most any objective person, didn't see that a crime had occurred—at least not by Flynn. It appeared, instead, that charges could be brought against some of the FBI agents. At the onset, Durham seemed curious as to why no one came forward and spoke up for Flynn. The answer came from William Henck, a former IRS attorney who was fired after thirty years on the job after blowing the whistle on a laundry list of shady IRS activities. Henck told Elizabeth Vaughn, a reporter for RedState, that the reason no one spoke up for Flynn was "No one in the FBI or the DOJ wanted to engage in a futile suicide mission that would put them and their families through years of hell, cost them hundreds of thousands of dollars, and put their pensions at risk, all so that their information could be ignored."[2]

Henck went through hell and had the people in a position to help Flynn spoken up, they would have gone through hell, too. But if more "Hencks" and "Sidneys" step up to push back, then maybe one day we can mitigate the risks of doing the right thing.

As for Flynn—what's the right thing? President Trump took the first step by pardoning him. Secondly, put the people who framed him in jail. Third, let him sue. Carter Page sued the DOJ, FBI, and several other people involved in Crossfire Hurricane for $75 million. How much would a Flynn lawsuit be worth? Does it matter?

How do you make someone whole when half the country thinks they're a traitor?

Read Flynn's words from his post-pardon statement and sear them into your brain, "Never again should any family or individual be so viciously targeted, maligned, smeared, and threatened such has been the experience of my family and I."

Never, ever forget—what happened to him could happen to you.

And *that* you should care about.

ACKNOWLEDGMENTS

When you're in the media business, you'll often hear friends and colleagues say, "I want to write a book." I used to be that guy. Then I wrote one. Then another. And let me clarify for those unaware—it is the hardest thing you'll ever do professionally. It is an "up at dawn and to bed at midnight," seven-day-a-week, arduous, and exhausting endeavor. However, the sense of accomplishment when you type that last period can't really be measured.

While it may seem a book project is basically one person at the keyboard, alone with their thoughts, a thirty-two-ounce cup of coffee, and a few notes, that's not really how it is. To use a very well-worn cliché, it takes a village, and I'm fortunate my village is a team of extraordinary people.

First and foremost, every good and perfect gift is from above, coming down from the Father of the heavenly lights. I am grateful to God for the gifts he's given me to do this, the desire to do this, and the opportunity to do this. Without Him, I have nothing, and I am nothing.

I'm so grateful for the incredible team at Post Hill Press, beginning with Anthony Ziccardi and Michael Wilson—my brother from another mother. This book exists because Anthony had an idea. He's like the Michael Keaton character, "Bill Blaze," in the film *Night Shift*, "I'm an idea man. I get ideas all day long. I can't control them. I can't even fight 'em!"

AZ had been wanting to find a project for me since I'd apparently impressed him with the last book I wrote—which I'd written for someone else. One day I got a call from Michael saying, "AZ woke up in the middle of the night and had an idea: 'Hey let's do a Flynn book! It'll be perfect for Erickson!'"

Little did I know I'd spend the next several months without an off weekend and just four hours' sleep every night.

Anthony and Michael have never wavered in their belief in my abilities, and I'm forever grateful for the opportunities they've given me. Managing editor Kate Monahan is one of the most patient people I have ever worked with. Thank you for that! To my editor, Monique Happy Pieniaszek, I thank you. I know it was a pain going through not one, but two manuscripts since I'd decided to add more content. When it comes to writing, like AZ, I'm a frenetic "idea man."

Without prayer, encouragement, and advice, I'd never be able to finish any project, much less one with the sheer volume of research this one required. Rayetta Sanchez, you are a faithful prayer warrior, and, boy oh boy, those prayers worked. When I needed a deadline miracle, you prayed, and it came to pass. Thank you! Chuck Wooten—a true patriot. I asked for prayer, you prayed; I asked for advice, you gave it. Truth be told, I see a lot of General Flynn in you. I am honored and proud to call you a friend. Judy Cocca, you know me well, better than almost anyone, and you know just exactly how to talk me off a ledge, although you probably wanted to *walk* me off a ledge a few times over the years. Kidding, of course. In all sincerity, your prayers and your calming words were more helpful than you likely know. Amy Carmen, your feedback was absolutely invaluable. Thank you! As my way of showing gratitude, I plan on learning how to play the opening guitar riff to the Raspberries' "Go All the Way" without butchering it, although, with apologies to Eric, that is highly unlikely.

Lastly, there are people in my life without whom I could never accomplish a thing. My daughter, Christina. She is the love of my life and the air that I breathe. Her sheer existence makes me want to be the best man I can possibly be. We may not agree on political issues, but I am forever proud of my beautiful muse.

My dad, Maurice. Let me tell you, he's the greatest man I know. He says what he means. He means what he says. And his word is his bond. When I sent Dad the last book I wrote, which was actually my first, he called me the day he finished reading it and said, "Wow! This is really good. I don't necessarily agree with every point you made in it, but your writing is fantastic!" That was everything to me.

My mom, Veronica. She's always been my biggest fan. Whenever I call, she's always, "So how's the book coming? I can't wait to read it!" Mom makes me feel like I'm her special guy, which I love as much as I love her. She believes in me, and I can't count the number of times she's invested herself into setting me up for success. Thank you, Mom. And yes, I am getting plenty of rest!

Laurie, wow, what can I ever say to convey how grateful I am for you?

Because of you, I get to do this. And I believe it's gonna be yuge!

You're my teammate, my partner, my love. The encouraging notes every day made this oft stressful undertaking a little more bearable, especially on the days I wanted to chuck it all, move to Belize, and sell Italian ice on the beach. They truly meant the world to me.

For months, you spent nights and weekends alone while I hovered over a computer keyboard. I know it wasn't easy. I'll make it up to you, I promise, and know this—I won't rest until Post Hill Press gives us the summer vacation we gave up!

Lastly, thank you General Flynn for your service. We live in the greatest country in the world, and I sleep better at night knowing patriots like you still exist. God bless you and God bless the United States of America.

ENDNOTES

ACT 1: WHO IS MICHAEL FLYNN?

1 Michael Flynn and Michael Ledeen, *The Field of Fight: How We Can Win the Global War Against Radical Islam and Its Allies* (New York: St. Martin's Press, 2017).

2 Ibid.

3 "Quick Thinking Saves 2 Girls," *Newport Daily News*, July 25, 1972.

4 Flynn and Ledeen.

5 Josh Krueger, "Middletown High School Athletic Hall of Fame Announces Its Class of 2016," *Newport Daily News,* August 20, 2016.

6 *Renaissance 1977*, University of Rhode Island Yearbook, University Archives. https://digitalcommons.uri.edu/cgi/viewcontent.cgi?article=1066&context=yearbooks (accessed June 15, 2020).

7 Flynn and Ledeen.

8 Ibid.

9 Ibid.

10 Marc Fisher, "The Partisan Warrior," *The Washington Post*, December 14, 2018.

11 Flynn and Ledeen.

12 Michael T. Flynn, Matt Pottinger, and Paul D. Batchelor, "Fixing Intel: A Blueprint for Making Intelligence Relevant in Afghanistan," *Voices from the Field*, Center for a New American Security, January 2010.

13 David Samuels, "The Aspiring Novelist Who Became Obama's Foreign-Policy Guru," *The New York Times Magazine,* May 5, 2016.

14 Flynn and Ledeen.

15 "Global Threats to National Security," C-SPAN, April 18, 2013.

16 Ibid.

17 Flynn and Ledeen.

18 Ibid.

19 Flynn and Ledeen.

20 Ibid.

21 Dana Priest, "Trump Adviser Michael T. Flynn on His Dinner with Putin and Why Russia Today Is Just Like CNN,." *The Washington Post*, August 15, 2016.

22 Arden Farhi, Margaret Brennan, Louise Dufresne, Josh Gross, Kathryn Watson, and Jacqueline Alemany, "A Timeline of Michael Flynn's Contacts with Russia, His Ouster and Guilty Plea," CBS News, December 2, 2017. https://www.cbsnews.com/news/michael-flynn-timeline-contacts-with-russia-ouster-guilty-plea (accessed August 7, 2020).

23 Paul Sonne, "Pentagon Finds It Has No Records Approving Mike Flynn's Russian-TV Pay," *The Wall Street Journal*, February 16, 2017.

24 Geoff Earle, "Disgraced Trump National Security Adviser Michael Flynn Was Paid $45,000 for Speech in Moscow at Dinner Where He Sat Beside Putin," *Daily Mail*, March 16, 2017.

25 Dave Gilson, "The Photo That May Help Unlock the Trump-Russia Scandal," *Mother Jones*, May 23, 2017.

26 Jeremy Scahill, "Intercepted Podcast with Jeremy Scahill: The Woman Democrats Love to Hate," *The Intercept*, June 7, 2017.

27 Ibid.

28 Priest.

29 Joshua Hersh, "Exclusive: Michael Flynn Regretted the 'Lock Her Up' Speech Almost Immediately," Vice News, July 6, 2017.

30 Morgan Phillips, "Pence Says He's Now 'Inclined' to Believe Flynn Didn't Intentionally Mislead Him about Russian Ambassador," Fox News, April 30, 2020.

ACT 2: SHADY STUFF THEY KNEW FLYNN WOULD UNCOVER

1 John Irish, "North Korean Nuclear, Missile Experts Visit Iran-Dissidents," Reuters, May 27, 2015.

2 Marc A. Thiessen, "Obama's Secret Iran Deals Exposed," *The Washington Post*, July 25, 2017.

3 Josh Meyer, "Obama's Hidden Iran Deal Giveaway," Politico, April 24, 2017.

4 Flynn and Ledeen.
5 Ibid.
6 Samuels.
7 Ibid.
8 Marc A. Thiessen, "Obama Took Lying to New Heights with the Iran Deal," *The Washington Post*, June 8, 2018.
9 Samuels.
10 Flynn and Ledeen.
11 Thiessen, "Obama's Secret Iran Deals Exposed."
12 Rich Edson, "Iran Has Fired 23 Ballistic Missiles Since Start of 2015 Nuclear Deal, Explosive Report Shows," Fox News, January 25, 2018.
13 Matt Apuzzo, Adam Goldman, and Nicholas Fandos, "Code Name Crossfire Hurricane: The Secret Origins of the Trump Investigation," *The New York Times*, May 16, 2018.
14 Ibid.
15 Michael S. Schmidt, Mark Mazzetti, and Matt Apuzzo, "Trump Campaign Aides Had Repeated Contacts with Russian Intelligence," *The New York Times*, February 14, 2017.

ACT 3: SLAUGHTER OF THE INNOCENT

1 Rowen Scarborough, "FBI Deliberately Hid Carter Page's Patriotic Role as CIA Asset, IG Report Shows," *The Washington Times*, December 11, 2019.
2 Josh Rogin, "Trump's Russia Adviser Speaks Out, Calls Accusations 'Complete Garbage,'" *The Washington Post*, September 26, 2016.
3 George Papadopoulos, *Deep State Target: How I Got Caught in the Crosshairs of the Plot to Bring Down President Trump* (New York: Diversion Books, 2019).
4 Ibid.
5 Jason Horowitz, "Rome University at Heart of Trump Inquiry Becomes a Vortex of Intrigue," *The New York Times*, October 14, 2019.
6 Papadopoulos.
7 Nicholas Kristof, "Is Hillary Clinton Dishonest?" *The New York Times*, April 23, 2016.
8 Papadopoulos.

9 John Solomon and Alison Spann, "Australian Diplomat Whose Tip Prompted FBI's Russia-Probe Has Tie to Clintons," The Hill, March 5, 2018.

10 Papadopoulos.

11 Mark Maremont, "Key Claims in Trump Dossier Said to Come from Head of Russian-American Business Group," *The Wall Street Journal*, January 24, 2017.

12 Shana Willis, "Jonas Savimbi: Washington's 'Freedom Fighter,' Africa's 'Terrorist,'" Institute for Policy Studies, February 1, 2002.

13 Kenneth P. Vogel, "Paul Manafort's Wild and Lucrative Philippine Adventure," Politico, June 10, 2016.

14 Willis.

15 Jeff Horwitz and Chad Day, "AP Exclusive: Before Trump Job, Manafort Worked to Aid Putin," Associated Press, March 22, 2017.

16 Ibid.

17 Natasha Bertrand, "Hacked Text Messages Allegedly Sent by Paul Manafort's Daughter Discuss 'Blood Money' and Killings, and a Ukrainian Lawyer Wants Him to Explain," Business Insider, March 21, 2017.

18 Evan Perez, Shimon Prokupecz, and Pamela Brown, "Exclusive: US Government Wiretapped Former Trump Campaign Chairman," CNN, December 10, 2019.

19 Andrew E. Kramer, Mike McIntire, and Barry Meier, "Secret Ledger in Ukraine Lists Cash for Donald Trump's Campaign Chief," *The New York Times*, August 14, 2016.

20 Rebecca Savransky, "Manafort Rips 'Unfounded, Silly' *NYT* Report," The Hill, August 15, 2016.

21 Rowen Scarborough, "Mueller Prosecutor Held Secret Meetings Targeting Paul Manafort Before Russia Probe: IG," *The Washington Times*, May 24, 2020.

ACT 4: CROSSFIRE RAZOR, A.K.A. "THE FRAME JOB"

1 "Biden: DOJ Dropped Flynn Case to Create 'Diversion' from Trump's Poor Covid19 Response," *Good Morning America*, ABC, May 12, 2020.

2 Alex Pappas and Catherine Herridge, "FBI Silent a Year After Senate Committee's Questions on Trump Tower Briefing," Fox News, September 4, 2019.

3 Chuck Ross, "John McCain Associate Had Contact with a Dozen Reporters Regarding Steele Dossier," *Daily Caller*, March 24, 2019.

4 David Ignatius, "Why Did Obama Dawdle on Russia's Hacking?" *The Washington Post,* January 12, 2017.

5 Carol E. Lee, Devlin Barret, and Shane Harris, "U.S. Eyes Michael Flynn's Links to Russia," *The Wall Street Journal,* January 22, 2017.

6 Mary B. McCord, "Bill Barr Twisted My Words in Dropping the Flynn Case. Here's the Truth," *The New York Times,* May 10, 2020.

7 Matthew Rosenberg and Matt Apuzzo, "Flynn Is Said to Have Talked to Russians about Sanctions Before Trump Took Office," *The New York Times*, February 9, 2017.

8 Greg Miller, Adam Entous, and Ellen Nakashima, "National Security Adviser Flynn Discussed Sanctions with Russian Ambassador, Despite Denials, Officials Say," *The Washington Post,* February 9, 2017.

9 Kevin Liptak, Jeff Zeleny, and Elizabeth Landers, "Trump Says He's Unaware of Reports Flynn Discussed Sanctions with Russian Ambassador," CNN, February 10, 2017.

10 Thomas J. Baker, "'Rewrite' in Flynn's Case Shows FBI Needs Reform," *The Wall Street Journal,* May 3, 2020.

11 Dan Boylan, "Michael Flynn Caught Up in Washington's Messiest Legal Drama in Decades," *The Washington Times*, May 15, 2017.

12 Cogan Schneier, "Litigators of the Week: Covington Pair Score the Plea Deal Read Round the World," *The Am Law Litigation Daily*, December 7, 2017.

ACT 5: THE TIDE TURNS

1 Gregg Re, "Mueller Memo Says Michael Flynn Has Provided 'Substantial Assistance,' Recommends Lenient Sentence," Fox News, December 4, 2018.

2 Sidney Powell, "POWELL: New Facts Indicate Mueller Destroyed Evidence, Obstructed Justice," *Daily Caller*, December 16, 2018.

3 Byron Tau, "Rift Deepens between Michael Flynn, Prosecutors over Cooperation," *The Wall Street Journal*, September 10, 2019.

4 Yael Halon, "Michael Flynn Attorney Responds to Explosive Documents: I Can't Even Tell You How Outraged I Am," Fox News, April 29, 2020.

5 John Gleeson, David O'Neil, and Marshall Miller, "The Flynn Case Isn't Over until the Judge Says It's Over," *The Washington Post*, May 11, 2020.

EPILOGUE

1 John Linder, "We Are a Nation of Laws, Not of Men," The Blaze, September 19, 2016.

2 Elizabeth Vaughn, "IRS Whistleblower Explains Why No One in the FBI or the DOJ Spoke Up for General Flynn," RedState, June 30, 2020.

ABOUT THE AUTHOR

Dave Erickson is an award-winning journalist, Emmy®-winning television producer, social commentator, and satirist. He's known for his biting wit and a fearlessness to say what people are thinking but are too afraid to say themselves.

The rest of Dave's résumé is on the back flap. Check it out. His picture is there and everything. It's easy to see Dave wishes he was a brooding rock star.

He grew up with parents who taught him the value of setting goals and working hard to achieve them. Dave's path in life was charted at the age of fifteen thanks to a visit to a local television station where he watched the production of a live newscast. That day he knew journalism, both in broadcast and print, was what he wanted to do with his life. He loved working on the television news team at his high school, with their small studio, control room, behemoth cameras, and a weekly broadcast on its closed-circuit system. Dave also launched the high school newspaper, which was *The Onion* before there was

The Onion. It was a satirical publication that, thankfully for him and his co-editor Craig, the school administrators never really understood enough to tell them to stop.

Dave landed his first professional reporting job at age seventeen, working at a small weekly community newspaper while still in high school. Quill and Scroll, the international high school journalism honor society, named him an "Outstanding High School Journalist." Back then he never could have known that there'd one day be publishing platforms like Twitter and the World Wide Web, and that the things he'd write on those platforms would be quoted by news outlets around the world.

After graduating high school and moving on to college, Dave picked up a love of radio and would later find himself working at an all-news station in Houston doing airborne traffic reports—his first big-market broadcasting job. That eventually led to reporting jobs in television and ultimately on-air commentary. Along the way, he'd also win accolades as a television producer.

Dave's focus would later change, bigly. As the country became more fragmented, especially after the 2016 presidential election, he felt an urgency to become more involved in the conversations shaping our country. Dave wasn't raised in a political home; in fact, politics was never discussed at home. But he saw how the America he grew up in was being pulled apart by people who hated it, and he determined if something wasn't done, America would be lost for good.

So, here we are.

On a personal level, though his career has taken him across the country, Dave loves everything about Texas, in particular Texas brisket, and he fancies himself a pit master, though the pit he masters is just an electric smoker in the backyard. He's a voracious reader, Food Network junkie (he's a Bobby Flay fanboy), wanna-be rock star, and currently the principal songwriter and guitarist for the techno-metal band "The Meese Commission."

Dave resides in Fort Worth, Texas with Laurie, their crazy but lovable rescue dog named Emmy, and a vast collection of books about AC/DC.